Human Energy

An Innovative Guide to Building a World-Class Business

Human Energy

An Innovative Guide to Building a World-Class Business

Joe Mosed

First Edition.

ISBN 13 Digit: 978-1-933598-79-6

Published by Johnson & Hunter, Inc.

Trademarks and References

*To my parents for planting the seeds
and my family for nourishing my soul.*

CONTENTS

PREFACE

The goal of any business is to attract and keep customers. Loyal, engaged customers bring more customers to you, and when this occurs your business will be on its way to greatness. The premise of this book is to create full engagement for all stakeholders including employees, management, and customers by harnessing human energy.

The issues that face business today are substantial in terms of resources, competition, and technology. An example is the power of social media. If you are connected to 172 people on LinkedIn, you have access to over 1 million people at the third level (if you are linked to John and John is linked to Mary, Mary is considered third level). Another example is lightning-fast communication flow. If your company screws up, people will know about it immediately.

There is also disconnect regarding the value of employees. "People are your greatest asset" is a popular belief; however if you walk into most HR departments and listen to the water-cooler conversation you will quickly find out that this is not true. Disengaged team members are, frankly, a pain in the ass and, according to a Gallup poll[1], they consist of up to 90% of your workforce. Actively disengaged employees account for 20% of that 90%—and they actually hurt the company.

Let me monetize this concept in the following example. Let's suppose you are a small organization with $25 million in annual revenue. To make the numbers simple, we will say you have 2.5 million impressions per year, which means your people talk to leads, prospects, and customers 2.5 million times a year. (This communication could be in any channel including face-to-face, email, social media, and phone.) Every impression is worth $10. If your disengaged employees control 500,000 of those impressions, you can assume they are negative and that they cost your company $5 million per year (500,000 negative impressions x $10 = $5 million). You can see there is a real and valid reason to improve the attitude of disengaged employees.

---

[1] Gallup, *Majority of Workers Not Engaged in Their Jobs*, October 2011
www.gallup.com/poll/150383/majority-american-workers-not-engaged-jobs.aspx

According to Gallup, fixing this will allow your
organization to grow 2.6 times faster than other
organizations. If you compound those results over a
five-year period you will become a market leader in your
segment. And, significantly, this happens without
increasing your costs because the impressions are
already there. You are simply changing and controlling
what happens with those disengaged employees.

Small- and medium-sized businesses are carrying the
weight of the U.S. economy and the goal of those
businesses is to create engaged customers. Engaged
customers cannot be created with a disengaged
workforce. If your business can double employee
engagement, you will double innovation and dominate
your market, which will result in more job creation.

This book ties team member engagement to customer
engagement. You cannot have customer engagement
with disengaged employees. The structure of the book
will start with the individual and progress to the
organization. I feel that you cannot build true team
member engagement if you don't care about your team.
In order to care about your people, you need to know
where they are at personally and professionally and what
they are wrestling with each day.

Putting a process in place to hire great team members and focusing on their engagement fosters customer loyalty. Customer loyalty is the number one driver for company growth which creates more jobs and a stronger economy.

What if you harnessed human energy effectively and slid the scales from disengaged team members to engaged team members? What would that do for your customers, stakeholders, and your business? My guess is it will transform your business into a world-class organization.

CHAPTER 1
THE IMPORTANCE OF UNDERSTANDING HUMAN ENERGY

A fulltime job allows us to satisfy most of our basic human needs. When employed in a good-paying job, people can afford food, shelter, safety, and are also more apt to be contributing members of their community. Jobs and employment are powerful forces in the world.

Small- and medium-sized businesses are responsible for most of the jobs in the United States; thus entrepreneurs have the potential of saving the U.S. economy. Entrepreneurs who create customers ultimately create jobs. Without businesses, there would be no tax base to support communities and education. If you look at my home town of Detroit, Michigan, you will see the effects of a booming economy and the results of a bust economy.

Henry Ford mastered the art of mass production and the car industry was born. His vision to create a mode of transportation that everyday Americans could afford changed Detroit. It also changed the world. Large corporations like Ford, GM, and Chrysler created ancillary businesses and thriving communities. People want to live in areas that provide good jobs.

When job creation is high, communities can afford public safety and other essentials. Safety is a core human need and when it is in jeopardy, people leave. Today Detroit is in a rebuilding phase and there are serious problems with safety, education, and job creation. The only thing that will spawn the rebirth of the Motor City is job creation. Job creation is a core requirement because tax dollars fund public safety and community improvements.

Being without work is devastating.

> John and Rebecca are married and have a young daughter. John has a college degree and is making a good living. They are building their family. John is laid off from his job and Rebecca, who is a part-time makeup artist, has to work more hours. They lose their home and have to rent because of the income slash. As time goes on, jobs are harder to find. John, being used to making $90,000 per year, finds it difficult to work for $12 an hour. Unfortunately 99 weeks pass and his unemployment runs out. Since there

are no executive jobs available, he is forced to take an hourly job. Thankfully John found one with benefits because Rebecca is diagnosed with a cancerous tumor.

There are several points to this fictional story. One is that scenarios like this are happening all over the country. Unemployment is high but underemployment is higher. And second, peoples' personal lives affect their work. To think not is to be naïve.

Remember, a successful business needs engaged customers and to have them you need engaged employees. When people are going through situations that rock the foundation of the Maslow Hierarchy of Needs (see Chapter 6), employee engagement becomes a myth.

Innovative Entrepreneurs are our brightest hope for fixing the economy. Knowledge based job creation is vital to our survival as a free nation. I cannot stress this enough. Job creation and business are the lifeblood of a healthy society.

Adolf Hitler began his ascent to power in Germany in 1919. World War I war reparations and other factors destroyed Germany's economy. Hitler was a charismatic orator and over time began to unite the people.

Desperate people will believe anything especially when there is perception of relief. Humans are driven to avoid pain and gain pleasure. Hitler understood those two motivations and almost took over the world. When an economy collapses, chaos ensues. The only remedy to avoid this is job creation. Joblessness creates hopelessness which is devastating to humans and spreads like wild fire.

Jim Clifton, the Gallup Chairman, wrote an excellent book titled *The Coming Jobs War*. One thing he writes about is Behavior Economics, the study of what people think before they do something. For example, what do you think about before you purchase a new car? Clifton says intention is something that can drain talent from companies and that people quit their jobs because of their direct managers. Once the thought of leaving crosses an employee's mind, the likelihood of him or her leaving increases significantly.

Where attention goes, energy flows. - Tony Robbins

Attention and intention are fickle things that are controlled by emotions first and intellect second. Understanding behavior economics will help entrepreneurs create customers, keep talent, and build businesses. Intention and circumstances have the ability to change lives.

> My childhood friend Chris lives in Las Vegas with his wife, Kary. For over 15 years, I would visit them a couple times per year. I always heard about Kary's sister Dana but in all that time had never met her. On one business trip, when I stopped by to visit, Dana happened to be in town. That chance meeting resulted in our marriage and beautiful twin girls.

Intention and circumstance have the power to change lives. If that business meeting had been in a different city, my intention to marry Dana would not have occurred.

CHAPTER 2
STARTLING STATISTICS

The competitive advantage for businesses today lies in the soundness of their business model. My software business is alive and well today because we spend an enormous amount of time on ours.

My company began as a reseller of business machines. We had a business-to-business selling model. In the tech business with a product price range of $10,000 to $500,000, the reseller model is a dying entity. We recognized this and decided to become an innovative software manufacturer. Once we did this, we focused on the distribution model. There are three things that create high value for software tech companies: intellectual property, the strength of the distribution model, and the recurring revenue generated. To prove the point, 80% of the S & P 500 value is created from intangibles like intellectual property, business model, and goodwill.

We understood that we had to sell direct so we could innovate faster. Being directly connected to the end user was critical for us to grow and innovate. Knowledge jobs are the key to creating customers and more jobs. Knowledge jobs exist in the creation of the product, marketing, sales, and services. This transition was not easy for the company but I recognized that we would be out of business in five years if we did not make these changes. Also, focusing on the business model removed the local sales barrier that was killing our company. When we were a reseller, we only sold in two states. When the financial crisis hit, we rethought our strategy and pioneered our remote selling model. This business strategy allowed us to sell nationwide and will allow us to scale worldwide.

The basis for a business model is understanding people. Do you understand the makeup of your workforce? Here are some statistics that will keep you up at night:

- The average American eats 158 pounds of sugar per year. Processed sugar creates mood swings and deep crashes.

- 33% of adults are obese

- 33% of high school graduates never read another book after high school

- 42% of college graduates never read another book after college

- There were 1.5 million NEW bankruptcy filings in the last 12 months

- Big pharmaceutical companies make billions of dollars each year on Ritalin, Prozac, Xanax, and other mind-altering drugs

- 43% of American families spend more than they earn

- Average households carry $8,000 in credit-card debt

- Average household income is $50,200 (household, not individual)

These are the people who run your business on the frontline and deal with your customers. Management theory and lofty mission statements don't help because they focus on the wrong end of the problem. It is difficult for a frontline person to focus on TQM (Total

Quality Management) if they are two weeks away from living on the street.

Below is an outline of Maslow's Hierarchy of Needs to demonstrate this point:

1. Air, food, and shelter

2. Safety, including protection and freedom from fear and anxiety

3. Love and being loved

4. Self-Esteem

5. Self-Actualization

The Maslow hypothesis states that the high needs—which are those at the bottom of the list—cannot be fully satisfied until the top needs are met. In today's economic and social climate, it is no wonder people are not performing at work.

The goal for your business is to implement a full-cycle plan with actions that can be MEASURED for your people to achieve phenomenal results. This is a bottom-up approach, which may seem counterintuitive to executives. The focus is on the typical frontline runners who speak directly to your customers (Remember the negative impressions example from above?). Let's see what happens if you can build a culture of continuous improvement for your team members.

For this example, I will use a customer service center consisting of team members and team leaders. Remember that your frontline team members and team leaders talk with your customers.

Let's suppose you have 50 people in your customer service center and the numbers break down as follows (please bear with me if you hate numbers):

1. $19 per hour average; working 40 hours per week

2. Total annual payroll = $19 per hour x 2,000 hours/year x 50 people = $1,900,000

3. Annual Revenue: $20,000,000

4. Annual Net Income: $2,500,000

5. Average revenue per employee: $400,000 (Note: S & P 500 is $880,000 per person)

6. Average income per employee: $50,000 (Note: S & P 500 is $96,000)

Let's see what a low 15% annual improvement would look like. The idea is to create a framework where this is attainable every year so the effects will be compounded over time. If each person in your firm can improve 15% per year then their effectiveness doubles in five years.

If you start with $20,000,000 in revenue and $2,500,000 in income, the picture looks like this:

End Year 1 Revenue: $23,000,000   Income: $2,875,000
End Year 2 Revenue: $26,450,000   Income: $3,306,250
End Year 3 Revenue: $ 30,417,500   Income: $3,802,188
End Year 4 Revenue: $ 34,980,125   Income: $4,372,516
End Year 5 Revenue: $ 40,227,143   Income: $5,028,393

This is the power and simplicity of focusing on small efficiencies on a short-term basis and compounding over time.

Can your people improve .29% per week? This equates to .058% per day improvement. In real terms, this means that if a customer service representative is responsible for 100 calls per day, he handles 115 per day by the end of the year. Incrementally, this is easy to take on and requires focus. The goal is not to have people simply work harder by beating them with a stick. The goal is to focus on the core task and make improvements so they can handle the 115 calls per day in LESS time. This is what you want to focus on.

What is the framework to get team members to focus on this 15% improvement? **Engagement** is the key to attaining these compounded results. To foster engagement, you need to understand what makes individuals tick and to hire the right people.

Think about oil. It must be found, drilled, transported, and refined before it finally becomes a valuable commodity. Refining oil is a process that sometimes goes off course, as in the BP disaster in the Gulf of Mexico.

I am not suggesting that employees are a commodity, but there are over 6 billion people in the world; thus, you can hire almost anybody. The goal is defining "right" for your purpose. What can you do to create the "right person" for the job? This is the heart of the matter for any organization that wants to outperform its competition. (*Hint: it is much easier to do the work and find the right person instead of trying to make a person right. I discuss this in more detail in Chapter 7 and Appendix C).*

HOW SELF-CONCEPT AFFECTS PERFORMANCE

Engagement in any task comes down to the individual, and a person's self-concept plays a significant role in this decision. Self-concept—the opinion you have about yourself—is programmed based on your environment, experiences, and opinions of others. Your self-concept is not truth but simply your opinion of yourself. This opinion dictates your on-the-job performance; that is people perform at the level they see themselves conceptually.

Self-concept can be reprogrammed based on the outcomes you want to achieve. However, **can you change your self-concept without changing yourself?** Answering this question breaks down a huge performance gap seen in most people.

> Pressure breeds resourcefulness even when resources are scarce. I was working for a tier-one auto supplier when my father asked me to join the family business. The business was a reseller of office machines. There was a rub: this business had three owners, two did not get along. At one time, they had all been friends. The only logical choice was either close the business or bring in new blood. Since two partners did not trust each other, the logical option was me. The conflict between the two partners created a ton of stress; so I told my father that I would only work with him if

the other two retired. He worked it out and we started working together.

My father passed away shortly after I joined the company. The pressure came in when I recognized that we had two important accounts, one was a manufacturer and the other was a distributor. These two accounts allowed us to buy at volume discounts without tying up our cash for too long. If we lost either one of these accounts the business would die. We had to transition or die. Luckily the transition worked because we lost both of those accounts and the business is stronger today than ever before. The moral of the story is that pressure breeds resourcefulness and the team members who made it work had the self-concept to perform under pressure.

Professional athletes deal with this kind of pressure all the time. We have seen unbelievable performances from the likes of Tiger Woods, Michael Jordan, and Peyton Manning. These individuals have a very strong self-concept regarding their profession and they have conditioned a winning attitude. These athletes win before the game is even played.

Rehearsal is a way to condition your self-concept so that any fear, uncertainty, and doubt are eliminated before the game even starts.

The short answer to "Can you change your self-concept?" is yes.

Before I discuss how to do it, let's talk about why to do it. Tony Robbins coined the formula LC = BP which stands for Life Conditions equal your Blueprint. When this happens, you are in harmony. When LC ≠ BP (Life Conditions are not equal to your Blueprint), you are unhappy. The blueprint is similar to a life plan. Here are some simple examples:

- I should be making $50,000 by age 25. I want to be married by age 30. I want my first house paid for by age 40. All of these are blueprints of what you think you should accomplish.

- The Life Condition is the reality. At 25, I am making $60,000. My life condition is better than my blueprint. I am 35 and not married. My life condition is worse than my blueprint.

The concept of life condition and blueprint works the same way for organizations. Basically it is a business plan that is tracked with actual results.

Breaking down your wants into buckets allows you to examine if your life conditions are in line with your blueprint for that area. Self-concept is one step above this formula because it dictates performance in all areas.

Do any of these statements ring true for you?

1. I am not good enough.

2. I am a loser.

3. I will never get that promotion.

4. I am not worthy of success.

5. I will do it tomorrow.

6. Money is the root of all evil.

Here are some additional questions that may identify negative self-concept and low self-esteem:

1. Do you have a genuine respect for yourself and who you are as an individual?

2. Are you happy with your personal appearance?

3. Are you ashamed or do you feel guilty about something you did?

4. Are you proud of your career and accomplishments?

5. Do you feel you do not have the social status you deserve in life?

6. Are you happy with your "inner person?"

7. Do you feel loved by your family, friends, and associates?

We all have negative thoughts at one time or another, but they should not dominate your thought pattern. If they do, changing your self-concept is a worthy goal.

Understanding the difference between your identity and your roles is the first major step in crafting your ideal self-concept. Separating your identity from your roles allows you to remove the emotional barriers that kill performance.

All inhibitions are learned. Babies do not have inhibitions. When you look at a baby, would you rate it a 1 (lousy) or 10 (excellent) as a person? The answer is 10. When it comes to identity, people are always a 10 and they will do everything to convince you that they are less than 10. This is because someone sold them on a false opinion. This does not mean that every behavior they do is a 10. Behaviors fall into roles that constantly fluctuate from 1 to 10. The identity and the freedom to react to any stimulus are always yours. No one can force you how to decide, and when you decide in a negative fashion your self-concept suffers.

Let's look at an example. You go on a sales call and the prospect informs you that he does not want to buy your product and that he is going to buy from your competitor. When you evaluate your performance after the call on a scale of 1 to 10, you rate your behavior a 5. On this particular day, your performance as a salesman was lousy. The point is that you are simply rating the behavior and not taking the poor performance personally.

Remember that you were born with an identity of 10. Don't let anyone talk you into a lower number. Understanding the difference between your identity and your business roles will allow you to control the negative self-talk and remove the self-limiting beliefs that hold you back.

How can you change your self-concept? There are several techniques to use; I will highlight three. These concepts are important because individuals work for organizations and interact with customers every day. Understanding what makes individuals tick is critical for improving your team and hiring smart, i.e., the right people for each job.

1. **Mentors** – Who do you look up to? Are there people who have achieved the life that you want? If so, study what they do and emulate their behavior. Leveraging other people's experiences is the fastest way to achieve goals. Why recreate the wheel when it already exists? Establishing mentors and emulating behaviors of people you hold in high regard is highly recommended.

2. **Imagination** – Albert Einstein attributed imagination over IQ when he discovered the theory of relativity. Using your imagination you can create your ideal self-concept. Remember that self-concept is simply your opinion of yourself. Decide on the opinion you want and crystalize it in your physiology through imagination.

3. **Invocations** – Invocations are routines that create a physiological change in your body's chemistry. Elite athletes typically establish routines so they can get into a high-performance state of mind. (For in-depth research on this, visit Tony Robbins website at www.tonyrobbins.com.)

Too often people tell themselves "I am not worthy of success." Self-sabotage is a problem that people may not even be aware of because it has been a habit for so long. Examining and controlling your self-concept is important if you want to achieve your goals. Creating a high-performance self-concept based on what you want out of life will elevate your accomplishments. Separating individual role behaviors from your identity allows you to have an objective view to improve your performance without beating yourself up.

There are real negative consequences for an organization that has team members with low self-concepts. Organizations cognizant of this fact realize negative attitudes spread like cancer and impact overall team performance. Organizations would be well served to focus on this with their existing team members and make sure their new hires have positive self-concepts.

GOALS AND SCORECARDS

Using a goal-tracking module for employees and the company is important. Typically this module should allow team members to create their own goals for their performance, which is public, as well as the option to create private goals.

Research shows that when companies care about team members' well-being, engagement improves. Providing tools for them to track health, wealth, and career goals is important to overall company performance. Likewise, having goals and tasks assigned and visible among the whole team brings a unified approach to this process.

Make sure the goal's interface is easy for team members to use and adopt. Also, track goal attainment and time so the whole organization can trend goal results.

Scorecards have been used in business for years. They have been effective at focusing talent on what matters. Establish a process so each team member has a scorecard and tracks his performance daily. This is important and often missed because scorecards typically show high level scores like profit per employee including revenue last quarter vs. plan rather than team member daily productivity.

For scorecards to become part of the company culture, they need to be relevant to each team member. Once you establish scorecards, you are enforcing a culture of high performance in your organization. Have a unified system to track performance and aggregate the results. Regardless if you use automated tracking or manual tracking make sure to implement a scorecard mechanic for every team member.

THE BRAIN

The human brain accounts for 2% of our body weight yet it consumes 20% of our total energy. Maximizing brain activity accelerates learning and fosters productivity. Understanding how the brain works is an important component to leveraging success and fulfillment. In John Medina's great book, *Brain Rules*, he outlines several methods for increasing the brain's effectiveness. Let's review the big three:

First, physical exercise boosts brain function. The brain operates on two things: glucose and oxygen. Consider that you can go 30 days without food, 7 days without water, but only 5 minutes without oxygen. Oxygen creates neural pathways in the brain, thereby improving function. Doing cardiovascular exercise such as biking, jogging, and swimming two days per week reduces the chance of Alzheimer's disease by 60%. This statistic by itself is worth the extra aerobic work. Your physical activities create enhanced brain wiring. Everybody is unique in this fashion; so it is important to understand your strengths and leverage them accordingly.

Second, sleep is a key factor in maximizing learning and brain function. During sleep, the brain is actively articulating and processing the knowledge gained from the day. Research shows poor sleep habits and lack of

sleep have negative effects on brain function.
Conversely, naps significantly improve brain function.
A NASA study conducted on pilots showed a 26-minute
nap during the day improved their performance by 36%.

> Polyphasic sleep is a concept of taking naps every 4 hours
> for no more than 30 minutes. It is estimated that a 30-
> minute nap has the same effect of 1.5 hours of sleep. Matt
> Mullenweg, the creator of Word Press blogging software
> used a polyphasic sleep schedule for one year when he
> created the software. He said it was the most productive
> year of his life.

Third, stress is the silent killer. Uncontrolled negative
stress caused by a sense of helplessness releases cortisol.
Cortisol is a survival hormone designed for fight-or-
flight response. It is designed for short bursts. Chronic
stress significantly increases cortisol levels and damages
the brain. Individuals and team members alike suffer
from stress-related issues at work. Stress and depression
are silent killers as well as financial killers. Depression
in the workplace costs U.S. companies an estimated
$200 to $300 billion per year.

Other factors that inhibit brain function and increase the
possibility of Alzheimer's and dementia are alcohol,
sugar, and a poor diet. Dr. Daniel Amen is a

psychiatrist, author, and medical director of the Amen Clinics. He uses SPECT Scan technology to show the differences between healthy brain activity and brains affected by bad habits. The good news is that you can reverse the negative effects on your brain by improving diet, exercise, and reducing alcohol use.

For more information on this type of brain research, check out Dr. Amen website at www.amenclinics.com

In summary, if you want to perform better in any facet of your life, you must take care of your brain and adopt a mentality of continuous learning. Learning is to the brain as exercise is to the body. A curious mind allows for growth and expansion.

In today's economy, these characteristics are required because most of the work requires creativity and thought. An open mind will allow you to perform better for yourself and your team.

Organizations that stake an interest in their team member's health continually demonstrate faster growth rates and more profitable returns.

THE BODY

Physical and mental energy have always been the Holy
Grail for me. Based on the amount of energy drinks,
coffee, and 5-hour energy shots that are sold each day, I
believe most people agree.

Is there a way to increase energy without these drinks?
The short answer is yes—but more importantly, is it
worth it? Let's look at some numbers and you can judge
for yourself.

According to the American Heart Association[2]:

Overweight and Obesity Stats for 2012

1. One in three American children ages 2-19 are
   overweight and obese.

2. The number of American children who are obese
   today is 5 times greater today than in 1973.

3. 149.3 million Americans ages 20 and older are
   overweight and obese. This is close to half of the
   U.S. population.

---

[2] http://www.heart.org/idc/groups/heart-
public/@wcm/@sop/@smd/documents/downloadable/ucm_319588.pdf

Costs

1. Total costs are estimated at $254 billion ($208 billion in lost productivity and $46 billion in direct medical costs.

2. Estimated costs by 2030 if current trends continue could reach $861 to $956 billion.

This is a real problem. Organizations are living with lost productivity every day and individuals battling obesity are dealing with low energy and low productivity.

Obviously diet and exercise are the answer to solving these problems and the wellness industry is now a trillion-dollar market. There are thousands of books, programs, and plans available that work—the main challenge is for people to consistently practice positive habits for the long term.

Let's examine how to solve this problem. The key to success is making a healthy diet and exercise a habit and lifestyle choice. Crash diets don't work in the long run and short-term goals are not effective. You may want to look good for your 20-year high-school reunion but what happens when the party is over? Typically, people slip back to their old habits.

What is needed are slight-edge daily changes that can have lifelong impact. Simple, small changes can have long-lasting and powerful results. Here is an example from Jeff Olson's book *The Slight Edge*. We will compare three friends who are basically the same weight and age. Jon decides to reduce his soda intake by one can per day, Mike decides to increase his intake of soda by one can a day, and Kevin will do nothing different. In this example one can of soda has 90 calories. (Note: one pound of body fat equals roughly 3,500 calories.) These are the results over a three-year period:

1. Jon loses 29 pounds.

2. Mike gains 29 pounds.

3. Kevin stays the same.

This simple change in daily behavior has roughly a 60-pound swing, which is why small, daily changes can have such a big impact. (Note: to burn roughly 90 calories, you have to walk 25 minutes.)

> If you work at home or have a flexible office environment, you can set up a treadmill and modify it simply with a shelf and an anti-static mat. Then, you can walk while working on the computer or reading. Humans evolved to be mobile and sitting eight hours per day in front of a computer has negative health consequences. Adding movement to your

day offers several benefits, like better blood flow, looser hip flexors which reduces back problems, and provides more energy. This simple setup has great results over time. Please note, you are not working out or exercising. You simply walk slowly while you work. I call it a "relax out" instead of workout.

Let's look at one more example. Food is used as energy and each organ in the body runs at an optimal megahertz (MHz) level. Normal brain function operates from 72-90 MHz. The rest of the body from the neck down has a frequency of 62-68 MHz. Sickness and disease start forming at 42-58 MHz and death begins at 25 MHz. Here is a general outline of MHz values of common foods (for detailed information, read *Sick and Tired* by Robert Young PhD):

1. Green Drinks: 250 MHz

2. Live Salad: 68 MHz

3. Fruits & vegetables: 15 MHz

4. Cooked hamburger: 5 MHz

5. Cooked Chicken: 3 MHz

The American Recommended Daily Allowance (RDA) is five servings of fruits and vegetables.

The goal is to maximize your energy and minimize impact so new habits are created. Becoming a vegetarian or vegan is not an easy task. The idea would be to simply substitute one green drink per day to boost energy and provide your body with the right nutrients needed to perform.

> I have made these changes to my diet. I enjoy eating and am not interested in becoming a vegetarian. Filling a water bottle with a green drink mix and water has helped me. It gives me an energy boost and eliminates bloating and acid indigestion. The gut is known as the second brain in terms of health; this simple daily habit change has worked wonders for me.

For long-term results with little impact on your daily life simply walk more during your NET time (no extra time). Take the stairs at work and stand up during conference calls. Doing simple things will compound into great results over time.

The result of doing nothing will cost your team members energy and your organization millions per year in lost productivity.

SELF-MOTIVATION

When individual motivations are focused and in line with organizational motivations, true engagement and customer loyalty are the outcomes.

Self-motivation is achieved by three things: autonomy, mastery, and purpose.

Autonomy

Autonomy is defined as independence or freedom, as of the will or one's actions. People want to be engaged as partners of the business. Autonomy is important because we are in a free society and people want freedom. The problem is that old-school management does not trust enough to encourage autonomy.

Examples of autonomy are flexible work schedules and working from home. If you have any experience dealing with creative people, then you know that people hit their "flow state" (see Chapter 4) at different times of the day. This can be difficult for managers to grasp because we have been conditioned to start at 8:00 AM (get in earlier) and leave at 5:00 PM (stay later). This creates the perception of hard work but it usually does not result in success for everyone. You can try a couple of things to test autonomy on your teammates. First, try a work-at-home day for a couple of your best people. If you see a performance improvement, then expand it.

Note: Autonomous team members must get their work done. You need to make sure the tasks are defined. Just because autonomy exists is NOT an excuse to slack off. You will find the opposite holds true. Autonomy will also build more trust with your people.

Mastery

The second tenant of self-motivation is mastery, the desire to get better at something that matters. Mastery is tricky because you must make sure your team members are in the right seat and doing the right job. Mastery can be a pain in the ass but it is a challenge that is rewarding because when it occurs engagement is at its highest level. Some things you can do to encourage mastery are to make sure your team members are good at what they are doing. Leaders need to probe and spend time with their team to make sure people are in areas that cater to their strengths. You do not want a person who sucks at detail work handling your accounting. Mastery is a quest and when people are working on the right things to master, then work and play become synonymous.

Mastery is seen by the likes of Bruce Lee in the martial arts, Mozart in music, and Warren Buffet in finance.

CHAPTER 2

Purpose

Purpose is the key to moving from C level work to A+ work. The most deeply motivated people who are most productive and satisfied hitch their desires to a cause larger than themselves. Dr. Frankel said it best in his award-winning book *Man's Search for Meaning*:

> "For success, like happiness, cannot be pursued; it must ensue, and it only does so as the unintended side-effect of one's dedication to a cause greater than oneself."

The first and most important concept regarding self-motivation is what I call "the compelling why." The *compelling why* is your purpose—the driving force behind your actions. It is why you were put on this earth.

Regardless of where you are in your career, you must know why you are doing what you are doing. This concept is so simple that it is often overlooked. If you hate the work you are doing, then understand it is simply a lesson of what you don't want to do long term. When you know the *compelling why* then bad jobs and crappy tasks can be viewed as stepping stones toward achieving what you really want. This positive mindset is required otherwise you will drift off track and become disengaged from your goal.

I realize this might be difficult to embrace for those new in their careers and making $10 per hour. But your *compelling why* is the motive behind doing what you love to do and becoming more of what you already are. As you move through your career, your *compelling why* will grow and change. The idea is for you to understand the why behind the what.

> *Know yourself and you will win all battles. –*
> *Sun Tzu*

Each job you have is a lesson, regardless if you love it or hate it.

> When I was young, I worked in landscaping, with asphalt, and on an assembly line. I can tell you that all of these jobs taught me great lessons. Being self-employed doing lawn work at fourteen taught me how to knock on doors, take criticism when doing a bad job, and collect money from deadbeat customers. The communication skills and gut lessons learned working this business for four years was more enlightening than my college education. Doing asphalt and cement work taught me the value of a hard day's work as well as showing me what I did not want to do as a career. Likewise, working at the Chrysler Jefferson Assembly plant was an outstanding experience that taught me many things including the lesson of not wanting to do it as a career.

If you don't know your *compelling why*, I suggest you read *Outwitting the Devil by* Napoleon Hill. In this controversial book, he discusses the difference between clear thinking and drifting. (I believe Hill was 50 years ahead of his time.) Andrew Carnegie pushed Hill to study success and failure—the result was this book and another one titled *Think and Grow Rich.* Hill's ideas are thought-provoking and eerily scary. *Outwitting the Devil* is a wakeup call and a course in psychology, making clear the working principles of the human mind. I ask you to keep an open mind, put your religious beliefs on the shelf, and read this book.

Think about life for a moment. For every action, there is an equal and opposite reaction. This profound law exists at every level: right/wrong, good/bad, rich/poor, hardworking/lazy, honest/dishonest. Life is a balance.

In *Outwitting the Devil*, Napoleon Hill wrote: "After 30 years of diligent snooping, found the Devil and wrung from him an astounding confession disclosing where he lives, why he exists, and how he gains control over the minds of people, and how anyone can outwit him."

Napoleon interviews the devil in full dialogue. The devil says he exists as the "negative part of the atom." This means he has to exist and is part of the human condition. Regardless of the religious connotations here, one thing is for certain: with success comes failure and failure success. Understanding that positive and negative exists in every facet of life is empowering once you free your mind from limitation and accept it as part of the ground rules for living. Being conscious of this fact is the first step to mastering it. In rudimentary terms, you cannot play football with a hockey stick. You have to understand the ground rules.

The devil reveals that he controls negative thought while God controls positive thought. "One of my cleverest devices for mind control is fear, the fear of poverty, criticism, ill health, loss of love, old age, and death." Do any of these fears sound familiar? These fears fall right into Maslow's Hierarchy of Needs which are physiological, safety, love/belonging, esteem, and self-actualization. The devil's fears hammer at the foundation of these needs.

The devil also says, "My greatest weapon over human beings by which I gain control of their minds, is the habit of drifting." A drifter is one who permits himself to be influenced and controlled by circumstances outside of his own mind. The greatest defense against this is thinking for yourself and free will. Free will is the greatest paradox of the human condition because you can choose to focus on negative or positive.

An example of drifting behavior is drinking one additional soda each day for three years. You wake up three years later and you have gained 30 pounds. Almost overnight you become overweight. As you know, habits work on autopilot regardless if they are good or bad.

Paraphrasing the Devil: "I cause people to allow me to do their thinking for them because they are too lazy and too indifferent to think for themselves."

Laziness + Indifference = Procrastination = Drifting

"Everything outside the minds of men is controlled by my opposition (God), by laws so definite that drifting is impossible. I control the minds of men solely because of their habit of drifting, which is only another way of saying that I control the minds of men only because they neglect or refuse to control or use their own minds."

The good news is that there is a prescription to avoid this. The following principles summarize what Hill has written in the aforementioned books and in *Laws of Success* and the *Master Key to Riches*.

1. Definiteness of purpose

2. Accurate thought

3. Mastermind

4. Controlling associations

5. Learn from adversity

6. Time is finite

7. Habit of doing more than paid for

Not having a *compelling why* can add up to a wasted life;
so, how do you find your purpose? The key is to control
your thoughts and your habits. Be aware of what is
happening and stop sleepwalking through life.

The first step in finding your **definiteness of purpose** is
to take notice of what your mind focuses on the most.
The idea is to leverage your strengths. From an early
age, I have always been interested in business. I would
talk for hours with my dad about different business
concepts. He was a serial entrepreneur; so I was lucky to
have him as a mentor.

Next, take an inventory of your thoughts. What does
your mind dwell on? Do you get fired up and passionate
about something?

Examine your good habits. When you are doing certain
activities, do you lose track of time? These activities can
be a gateway into what you love to do. Think about
what puts you in a flow state.

Lastly, what is it that people ask of you? Do you find that people lean on you for certain things? This could be a sign that you are innately good at that.

To crystalize the importance of a *compelling why*, let's look at other people who knew what their purpose in life was:

> *We are here to put a dent in the universe. – Steve Jobs*

> *The meaning in my life is to help people find meaning in theirs. – Dr. Viktor Frankel*

> *Being unwanted, unloved, uncared for, forgotten by everybody, I think that is a much greater hunger, a much greater poverty than the person who has nothing to eat. – Mother Teresa*

> *A free world-class education for anyone anywhere. – Sal Khan KahnAcademy.com*

Accurate thought is a requirement for self-motivation and success. For example, a business pays taxes and creates jobs but the goal of a business is to create shareholder value. Since the owners are taking a risk, they need to make a return. This is the essence of the

Free Enterprise System and it is why we get to enjoy so many things. Accurate thought is required because the market does not care if you need a new house or a new car. The market will only provide you these things if you deserve them.

Mastermind groups are powerful. Organizations that harness energy in the form of great teams can dominate any market. A Mastermind group filled with team members consisting of different strengths and experiences can create unbelievable results. Likewise, for the entrepreneur starting out in business, a good Mastermind group can shave decades of time and allow you to get results quickly.

Be careful to whom you listen to. **Controlling your associations** is one of the best pieces of advice I have received. Positive associations will take you down the path to success fast. You can shave off years of hard work by associating with people who have already done what you want to do. Likewise, the inverse is true. If you associate with the wrong people, your success can be derailed. This is common in sales. There is no easier field to measure performance than sales. You either hit your numbers or you don't. Most organizations live by the 80/20 rule which means 20% of your sales force brings in 80% of the revenue. This means the other 80% of the sales force you don't want to associate with. If you want to be successful in sales, then associate with the 20%. A negative mindset in sales will guarantee failure.

Learn from adversity. Thomas Edison tried thousands of filaments for the light bulb before he found the right one. Each filament that did not work was a learning experience. Learn from your mistakes.

Time is finite. You can do three things with time: spend it, invest it, or waste it. Protecting your time and focusing on your Definiteness of Purpose are required for success and happiness. Organizations deal with this on a collective level. The organization that harnesses the collective time of its workforce toward agreed-upon goals will outshine its competitors and dominate its market. Focusing time and attention on purpose is the key to individual and organizational success.

The habit of doing more than what you are paid for is a simple concept. When you buy something, you do so because of the perceived value it will bring to you. Sharp entrepreneurs know that value sells. It has nothing to do with price.

The same holds true if you are an employee working for somebody. If you continually want more money and responsibility then deliver more than what you are paid.

Good managers and business owners know how to spot value. If you adopt the habit of doing more than you are paid then you will always be valuable to your organization.

41

CHAPTER 3
THE FOUR ENERGY TYPES

Although organizations must fill the right seats with the
right people, it is the responsibility of the individual to
commit to maximizing his/her output. Great
organizations cannot be created if people avoid
accountability and the responsibility of maximizing their
engagement.

In *The Power of Full Engagement*, Jim Loehr and Tony
Schwartz outline four energy types—Physical, Spiritual,
Mental, and Emotional. Understanding and maximizing
these energy types is key for you to maximize your
engagement in life and at work.

PHYSICAL ENERGY

Physical energy is the bedrock of all energy sources.
Let's face it, without good health, nothing else matters.

You cannot perform well if you do not take an active, responsible role in your health.

To keep the body in good health is a duty ... otherwise we shall not be able to keep our mind strong and clear. - Buddha

Health is a flighty concept because typically people do not consider it until it starts to decline which is why 80% of the healthcare costs in the U.S. are spent in the last 20% of people's lives.

Taking control of your physical health is required to maximize the other three energy sources. Simple things like exercise, breathing, naps, eating right, and drinking water are required for good physical health. Investing in these simple activities breeds positive results.

It is not the amount of time you spend on something that makes you engaged but the amount of effort and energy you put into the activity that fosters high performance.

SPIRITUAL ENERGY

The human spirit is what keeps you going through good times and bad. Spiritual energy is released when you focus on things bigger than yourself. Emerson's Law of Compensation simply states that if you want more then you must give more. Living to a higher purpose driven by meaning and compassion is the key to maximizing your spiritual energy.

Spiritual energy can be harnessed at the organizational level. Good leaders know that a compelling vision and purpose statement focuses energy toward a goal. An excellent example of harnessing spiritual energy at the organizational level is www.Toms.com (they sell shoes and eyewear). For every pair of shoes sold, they donate a pair to people in need. On their website it states: *"With every pair you purchase, TOMS will give a pair of new shoes to a child in need. One for One."*

> *Purpose captures and holds attention. – Joe Mosed*

You need to examine your core values and decide what is meaningful to you. Working in a job you hate drains your physical and spiritual energy and kills the spirit of the organization. Managers need to flush this out and help people find what they are looking for.

Warren Buffett said: "Really getting to do what you love to do every day—that's really the ultimate luxury. And, particularly when you get to do it with terrific people around you." This simple statement sums up spiritual energy and fulfills the human need for self-actualization.

Mental Energy

Mental energy is important, especially for right-brain creative work. Maximizing concentration and focus are required to produce maximum performance and achieve your desired outcomes. The brain functions like a muscle; if you do not use it, it atrophies. Continuous learning and constant gaining of knowledge maximizes your mental energy. To break through levels and show improvement requires resistance. Resistance causes short-term frustration but yields long-term results. The same is true when you are learning something or trying to push past a physical barrier. (If you ever ran a marathon, you will understand resistance.) The same holds true with learning.

> To build my business, it is required that I read. When I lost my dad early in my career, I also lost my sounding board and business mentor. So I turned to books. When I graduated from high school, my reading level was below the sixth grade. (I am not sure how I was accepted at Michigan State. Perhaps they needed the tuition.) As an adult, when I had a compelling reason to learn, I was forced to get better at reading. Reading was always difficult for me because it was too slow and my comprehension was horrible.

> To bridge this gap, I took an interest in technology to increase reading speed. I studied speed-reading, mental photography, and photo-reading. All of these courses helped and through short-term resistance and sheer determination, I was able to increase my comprehension and reduce reading time from an average of 10 hours on one book to one hour. The moral of the story is resistance is a good thing when the long-term goals are kept in mind.

EMOTIONAL ENERGY

According to the Laboratory of Neuro-Imaging at UCLA, humans are blasted with 70,000 random thoughts per day. These thoughts are positive and negative. The best way to maximize emotional energy is to control the negative thoughts and turn them into productive use.

I am not simply advocating the use of positive affirmations. Positive affirmations without action lead to delusion. The human brain contains mirror neurons which is why kids do what you do and not necessarily listen to what you say. Mirror neurons are required for survival. The problem is that Americans on average watch 35 hours of TV per week. This does not include the time surfing the web and playing videogames. This activity has a huge influence on emotional energy. According to Mihaly Csikszentmihalyi, a psychology professor and former head of psychology at the University of Chicago, TV is a passive task and is shown to create anxiety and low-level depression. Csikszentmihalyi is best known as the author of *Finding Flow and Flow.*

Harness your negative emotions and control them by having the long-term view in mind.

> A little bird decided to wait to fly south for the winter. The rest of the flock left and he waited. The weather was still very nice. One day it got cold so he started on his journey south. As he was flying, his wings froze and he crashed to the ground. All of a sudden a cow walked by and went number two on top of him. The bird was furious but then his wings started to thaw. He began to sing because he was happy. A cat heard the singing and walked up to the bird. The cat was very nice and began licking him clean. The bird was excited because he would soon be flying south again. However, before he could start flying, the cat ate him.

There are several morals to this story. One, don't procrastinate. Two, your perceived enemies may be doing you a great service (the cow). Three, your perceived friends may be doing you a great disservice (the cat). The point is to control your emotions by having a long-term view that will allow you to maximize emotional energy.

If you are skeptical about the power of these four energies, let's look at some stats. According to the book *Power of Full Engagement*:

1. In a study of 80 executives over a nine-month period, those who worked out regularly improved their fitness by 22% and demonstrated a 70% improvement in their ability to make complex decisions as compared with non-exercisers.

2. At Union Pacific Railroad, 75% of employees reported that regular exercise improved their concentration and overall productivity at work.

3. The Coors Brewing Company found that it got a $6.15 return for every $1 invested in a corporate fitness program.

4. Equitable Life Assurance, Motorola, and General Mills reported a $3 return for every $1 invested in a corporate fitness program.

In summary, all energy types maximized will foster full engagement. Individuals need to take responsibility for their own engagement and organizations need to make sure each team member is engaged. This starts by having caring managers, and it also means that managers should fire people who are actively disengaged, even if they like them. When people are actively disengaged, they are wasting their time and the organization's time and the manager is doing them a great service by helping them find what makes them happy. Short-term resistance will cause frustration but that is what creates growth.

> *It is the mind that quits first. – Arnold Schwarzenegger*

CHAPTER 4
THE IMPORTANCE OF FINDING FLOW

INDIVIDUAL FLOW

The best advice I ever received was simply this: do what you love. The problem is sometimes life gets in the way. You have to work to support your family and pay your bills; then you find yourself trapped in a job that is not satisfying. Gallup[3] statistics shows this to be true as 90% of the workforces are disengaged.

Flow is the state of mind when you lose yourself in the performance of a task. Musicians play music, artists create art, and elite athletes play. In all these scenarios, the task is part of the person. Bridging work and play into the same activity is the essence of flow. Flow tasks

---

[3] Gallup, *Majority of Workers Not Engaged in Their Jobs*

are rewarding—knowing what puts you in flow is half the battle to success.

How do you know when you are in a flow state? Pay attention to activities that cause you to lose track of time.

Flow is not a passive state. You are not in flow when watching TV or sleeping on the couch—although when you are in a flow state you can be very relaxed.

Flow is active. Jim Rohn, the great business philosopher, said: "Make relaxation a necessity not a goal. Life is for enterprise. We must all wage an intense, lifelong battle against the constant downward putt. If we relax, the bugs and weeds of negativity will move into the garden and take away everything of value."

One way to investigate flow is to take an inventory of your good habits. What is it that you find yourself routinely doing? Do you build things, garden, exercise, or write software? Your rituals will lead you to find your passion. Pay attention to the time of day you typically find yourself in the zone. Are you most creative in the morning or at night?

Let's look at some examples. Habitual exercise is a good indication of a flow state. I exercise in the morning. My routines are at least 30% more effective if

I do them first thing upon waking up. Exercising at night causes my performance to suffer significantly. Writing is the same. On highly productive days, I wake up at 3:00 AM and load up on coffee and write. I can get more done in the space of two hours then I would in ten hours after lunch. In my profession, we make enterprise software. I have software professionals that have the opposite flow time. They start hitting their stride at 11:00 PM. Typically they get wired and do coding night-benders to get high-functioning tasks completed. So, think about what time you perform the best.

Another idea behind flow is leveraging your strengths. Usually when you are very good at something, you tend to enjoy it. Take an inventory of your strengths and if you lose time in those activities then you have identified your flow state.

Flow is critically important for organizations and individuals. Organizations that have what I call "Organizational Flow" have successfully harnessed the flow states of their team members into a grandiose purpose. The *compelling why* of these organizations creates excellent purpose as well as a healthy balance sheet. Companies that excel at this are Apple, Amazon, Facebook, and Google.

ORGANIZATIONAL FLOW

Organizational flow is the Holy Grail for business.
When your organization is in flow, you are growing,
your team members are fully engaged, and you have
loyal customers. Attaining organizational flow can be
like pulling teeth with pliers. The reason for this is that
businesses that grow have one thing in common: people.
Aligning people to achieve organizational flow in
today's economy is hard work, hence this book.
However, it is worth the effort, as seen by the following
examples of organizations that have achieved it.

*Apple was dying until Steve Jobs came back. He
borrowed $150 million from Microsoft and was off to
the races. He killed products, created new ones, moved
people, fired some, and hired others. He created a
culture larger than himself and recruited team
members who wanted to make a dent in the universe.*

*KhanAcademy.com is a free online website that is
revolutionizing education. Sal Khan, the founder,
identified that learning is universal and all people
should have access to world-class education for free.
Everybody who works for KhanAcademy.com
understands this purpose and strives to hit it.*

*The Pittsburg Steelers dominated football in the 1970s.
Players like Terry Bradshaw, Mean Joe Green, and
Franco Harris are idealized by millions of fans to this
day. They won four Super Bowl championships in six
years. Every team member from the towel boy to the
owner needed to be aligned and in flow to pull off this
record. Professional football is one of the most
competitive professions in the world and this record
could not be accomplished without organizational flow.*

I think the why behind organizational flow speaks for
itself. Let's examine how to achieve it.

Investing time in your team is critical if you want to
achieve organizational flow. Making sure your team
members are in the right jobs that utilize their unique
strengths is how you achieve organizational flow. In
theory this is a simple concept but putting it into play
requires work, dedication, and a passion for discovery.

Front line managers have the power to achieve this in
short order if they simply do three things: first, they must
trust their people. Second, they must give their people
tangible daily measures of performance; and third, they
must identify the meaning behind each job and define
who depends on their work and why. This will not work
if the top-brass executive management runs a

dictatorship. The idea is to raise employee engagement to foster customer loyalty.

CHAPTER 5
REWARDS

Can monetary rewards actually have a negative effect on performance? Is task performance intrinsically motivating? There is a disconnect between what science knows and business does. Daniel H. Pink wrote *Drive,* a great book that dives into this in detail. Let's review some key points from his work.

Pink says if you are responsible for growing an organization, then getting motivation right is critical for employee engagement. Companies with engaged employees grow 2.6 times faster than other organizations (according to Gallup[4]). Old-school motivation tactics need challenging in today's market place. The carrot-and-stick mentality of reward and punishment no longer works in the information age and can be a talent drain.

[4] Gallup, *Majority of Workers Not Engaged in Their Jobs*

Left-brain work is structured and repetitive. Right-brain work is creative. An example of left-brain work is to make 100 parts per hour for eight hours. Right-brain work would be to create a new software module. Work that requires continuous thought needs a new motivation standard.

Eighty-nine percent of the Fortune 500 value is created from intangible assets. These assets are created from thinking (right-brain work). They include intellectual property, business models, goodwill, and customer relationships.

If you are a company leader or manager, you need to scout your talent pool and make sure everyone is in the right position. The wrong positions kill purpose. The work and the ends have to have a purpose larger than the individual. The long-term effects will result in prosperity.

RECOGNITION AND APPRECIATION

If money is not the main motivator, how do you reward your people?

Gary Chapman wrote revolutionary books on relationships and appreciation *(The 5 Love Languages* and *The Five Languages of Appreciation).* In a nutshell, they outline how people express and receive love, the issues when people don't know each other's love language, and how to show appreciation. Once you understand these concepts you can translate them into the workplace.

Payroll is the biggest expense for almost every business. If you want to grow a successful organization you need employees. According to Gallup[5], an organization with engaged team members grows its earnings 2.6 times faster than organizations with disengaged employees. This is a big deal because you can suffocate your competition by beating them to the market and simply grow an excellent business through engagement. Engaged team members create engaged customers who create loyalty and more customers.

---

[5] Gallup, *Majority of Workers Not Engaged in Their Jobs*

CHAPTER 6
MASLOW'S HIERARCHY OF NEEDS

Dr. Abraham Maslow was known as the father of humanistic psychology. He hypothesized that human needs build on top of each other in a pyramid like fashion. The basic needs build the base of the pyramid with things such as food, shelter, and oxygen. These are the necessities of life. The top of the pyramid is self-actualization which highlights achieving individual potential.

You can see there are universal human needs and when you align these needs to organizational performance then you can achieve organizational flow and "organizational actualization." These universal human needs of freedom, competence, and belonging are vitally important.

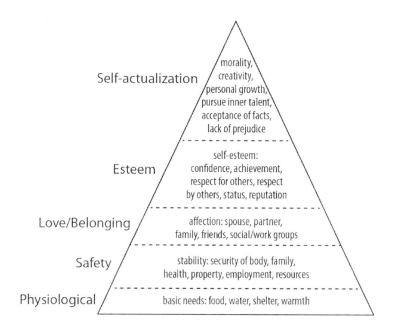

Let's examine what happens when these needs are not met.

Dictators try to operate and control human energy similar to a beehive. Basically you have the queen bee and all the worker bees creating and sustaining life. In a true Republic, man is free and controls his own human energy. How does this relate to progress and organizational actualization? The most effective comparison you can make would be to look at East Germany and West Germany after World War II. When the Cold War ended, the Berlin Wall came down and

East Germany found itself 40+ years behind West Germany. Centralized power cannot control human energy effectively. Progress is always stifled. This is why some of the cruelest dictators are at the heart of poverty and famine. You can simply look at Sudan and Libya for proof.

Natural law is competitive. If you examine nature in detail, you will see this. The food chain and survival are based on competition. The zebra runs for its life while the lion chases it for dinner. How does this affect human energy and self-actualization? Simply this, genius thrives on rivalry. If you look at all great victories in the past, you will agree that rivalry is critical for achieving great success. Here are some examples: Sea Biscuit and War Admiral; Muhammad Ali and Joe Frazier; Secretariat and Sham; George Patton and Rommel. This also works in business. The sales profession is probably the best naturally competitive field because there is no second place. You either win or go hungry.

Human energy flourishes with free will. We cannot force people to do anything. It is now known that the pyramids in Egypt were, in fact, created with free labor not slave labor. Historians know that nothing could be created that perfect under slave conditions. The ingenuity that comes out of the U.S. is still the best in the world. People are free to tinker in their garages and work on what they want to solve. Free will is the key to innovation.

A Cornell University study looked at 320 small businesses and tracked their performance. Half of the businesses were run from a command-and-control mindset and the other half granted autonomy throughout the workforce. The businesses that granted autonomy grew four times faster than the businesses that did not and had a third less turnover. These are compelling results.

> *Tell the people what to do and let them do it. They will surprise and surpass your wildest expectations. – George S. Patton*

CHAPTER 7
MANAGEMENT AND TEAM MEMBER
ENGAGEMENT

Good and effective management requires hands-on interaction with your people. In *Good to Great* Jim Collins says it is Level 5 Leadership that separates good companies from great companies. Management directly influences team member engagement; leadership does not. Most team members are simply treated as cogs on a wheel and not as parts of a team, which further disengages them from the organization.

Let's examine three things managers can do to foster employee engagement. First, managers have to know their people and take an active interest in them. This is simply common sense, but most management structures do not promote this behavior.

Would you invite your neighbors to your home if you did not like them? Why in the world would you spend 30% of your life with people you do not know or like? Being known and belonging is a basic human need.

Managers need to know their direct reports. The reason most managers are not comfortable with this is simply because they feel they cannot hurt their friends. How do you work with somebody you sincerely like and then wake up one day and fire them? This is a valid question, but the math simply does more harm than good. Let me illustrate through example.

If Johnny works for you for five years and you kept him at arm's length then you really do not know his strengths, interests, and passion. You invested 1,825 days being cautious for the one day when you might have to fire him. This is a bad investment and a huge waste of time. How can you leverage Johnny's strengths if you really don't know what they are? Getting to know Johnny is a good investment for you, your department, and the company.

Since we are on the subject, let's examine why people get fired. Typically people get fired for active disengagement, bad performance, or maleficence. That's it. The two areas you can influence are engagement and performance. I postulate that active disengagement

simply arises when people are in the wrong position.
There is a strong need in companies for critical mindsets.
Financial personnel and creative engineers need to have
a critical mindset toward the status quo. A great
example of this was Steve Jobs. He was critical of
everything and difficult to work for. This mindset of
annoyance built one of the most successful companies in
the world. On the flipside, if this mindset is customer-
facing then you have grounds for termination. If a team
member becomes actively disengaged, firing him is a
blessing. The reason for this is he is not happy and he
will absolutely find a different job.

This outlook is important because if you have a good
friend who works for you and he hates it, it is up to you
to encourage him to leave. Actively disengaged people
are cancers to the organization and it is up to
management to take care of it. Get to know your people
and take an active interest in them. The payoff
outweighs the cost one hundredfold.

The second tenant of how management can foster
engagement is that all team members' performance must
be measured. How do you know if someone is not
performing unless you measure his behavior? You
don't. Bad performance becomes merely subjective.

A core human need is self-actualization and the mastery of performance. In order to master something, you have to measure it. How do you put this into practice? Using scorecards is a great tool. It is management's responsibility to detail which aspects of the job are measurable, convey the expected performance criteria to employees, gain buy-in, and then establish the procedure for monitoring and how often it is reported and the data acted on. Managers need to work with their direct reports and make sure they are measuring the right behaviors.

The third component to full engagement is relevance. All team members need to know how their job is relevant to the organization. Jobs that are customer-facing are straightforward because they have direct impact to customers. The back office jobs are a bit harder to quantify. Managers who invest their time to qualify how each position is relevant to the company will enjoy the payoff.

> In our organization, Mo does the bill collecting. On the surface, this can be a thankless job because calling people for money is not pleasant. However this function is very relevant to our organization. You can build the best product, sell millions of dollars' worth of it, and provide the greatest customer service on the planet but if you do not get paid then you end up in bankruptcy. The relevance of

> accounts receivable to team members is hugely relevant.
> Do your AR people know their relevance?

If you run your department at arm's length, you will never get full potential from your people. It is a much greater gift to fire friends if they hate their work or perform badly. This is a telltale sign of unhappiness and disengagement. Giving them the freedom to do something else is a gift.

Rethink your strategy about people if you are not close to your direct reports. This could mean the difference between active full engagement and active disengagement. Your bottom line will thank you.

A great book on this subject is *The Three Signs of a Miserable Job* by Patrick Lencioni.

TEAM MEMBER ENGAGEMENT IS CRITICAL FOR SUCCESS

Organizational success is based on profit. This does not mean contribution and storied vision are not important, but an organization will not live without profit. Profit is maximized by employee engagement and customer engagement. Those two components will lead to profit—assuming the business model is sound.

Creating a culture of team member engagement requires planning. **Do you have a clear plan and direction for the company, department, project, and position?** Think about this question for a moment because it is loaded.

THE IMPORTANCE OF HAVING A PLAN

Organizational direction is usually created by the founder or CEO. This is the main rudder on the ship but all of the other areas must have the same plan and direction or the ship is powerless and will not move.

In the organizational chart on the following page, I propose the customer is the only one that pays the bills. The CEO/business owner must work to empower the team to perform for the customer. The business owner must establish processes and procedures that let the team deliver for the customer. This is why the business owner is also at the bottom of the chart. Empowering the team to perform with the customer in mind is the fastest way to profitable growth. This is a different mindset but companies that execute it build a solid reputation and profound profit. (Consider the profit and growth of companies like Apple and Zappos.)

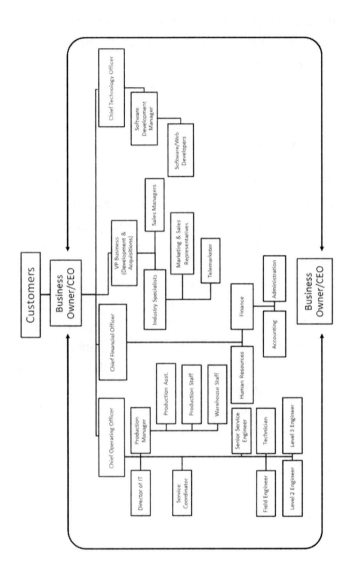

Let's examine the individual position. People are hired all the time with no real direction or plan for the position. Typically the department manager recognizes that people are busy and they need help. Thus staffing increases along with payroll. Also, people get hired in for one thing and end up doing another. Here is an example.

> I went to work for a Tier 1 automotive manufacturer in the sales department. For the first week I sat at a desk looking for something to do. Finally, I became a paper pusher doing forecasting for volume of car models. This function was created to help manufacturing estimate the number of parts they were going to make. As time went on, I became customer facing, talking with the buyer of our biggest customer, Ford Motor Company. I had no training and no supervision on the company, its plan or direction and I was talking with the lead buyer of our biggest client. This is a scary fact that happens every day in the business world. Management left me with the keys to the castle and hoped I would do a good job. This is like performing major surgery for the first time with no supervision or oversight. This happened because everybody was too busy doing other things. This begs the question: Too busy doing what?

There are some good points to this story. First, the freedom to do a job is vitally important for growth and was a huge perk. Second, this allowed me to reap more responsibility quickly which was something I wanted. The drawbacks, however, could have been devastating. I had to learn the manufacturing process to communicate to our customer. This was done by raw determination. I walked our manufacturing floor and asked a ton of questions from the people doing the work. They were kind enough to show me the ropes. The information garnered from the self-learning proved fruitful for this customer.

This method of learning—OJT (on-the-job training)—is common in companies, especially small businesses. Smart organizations will not let this happen. Defining every position's requirements is essential. This does not translate to fully scripting the job. It simply means that skill sets and performance metrics are known before the position gets filled. If this is not done, then matching employee skill sets to the required performance and position skill sets required is no different than asking a blind person to direct traffic. The failure percentage is higher than 50% and usually fixing the problem takes some time which leaves plenty of opportunities to create customer dissatisfaction.

Classic manufacturing management was very process-oriented which revolutionized manufacturing as a whole. This created enormous wealth for the American economy. Eliminating waste, measuring every step with time studies, and cutting the fat out of the supply chain is brilliant for left-brain work and repetitive tasks. Using this method for creative right-brain work is disastrous. You simply cannot manage creative people using this method. Creative work needs autonomy and purpose, and must create extreme value. The system for creative work cannot entail a lot of bureaucracy.

Let's look at Apple as an example. Apple designs all of its products in California and assembles them in China. This shows that the creative work cannot be outsourced while the manufacturing work can be.

THE EFFECTS OF MANAGEMENT STYLE

Dictator-style management is another example of old-school methods. History shows that progress and wealth are created in free societies while tyranny and poverty plague dictatorships. To a lesser extent, this happens in companies as well. If we profile Lee Iacocca's rescue of Chrysler Corporation, this is apparent. Back in the 1970s and 80s Chrysler was close to bankruptcy and received a government bailout. In this scenario, initial direction from the top down was needed to save the company. Decisions needed to be made to get the company back on track. Mr. Iacocca executed on the plan and saved the company. The failure came after the loans were repaid. The innovation stopped because

Chrysler had a full army but only one commander. Ego and other narcissistic traits started to fill the spotlight for Chrysler's main general. Over time, Chrysler fell into trouble again. The lesson is simply that dictator-style management does not work to create long-term sustainable value because the dictator did not invest in having a competent leadership team. Therefore, there is nobody left to take the reins of the company. Organizations that create products and innovative software will find its talent drained using this type of management strategy.

Jim Rohn, the great business philosopher, said that the American free enterprise system is a ladder. This is a great analogy because people move up the ladder based on skills, knowledge, and talent. Companies taking this into consideration will foster additional employee engagement. Upfront career planning between the company and the team members will help eliminate the Peter Principle which states that people are promoted to their level of incompetence. When company leaders focus on long-term career planning, they need to address added responsibilities and monetary growth.

Position strengths need to equal employee strengths. When these are not equal, mediocrity is assured. Eighty percent of the S & P 500 value is tied up in intangible assets. These include intellectual property, branding, talent, business model, customer engagement, and team member engagement. All of these assets are created with right-brain creative thought.

THE BENEFITS OF METRICS

Empowered teams are focused on metrics and outcomes. The three core components of any business are employees, customers, and profit. Focusing on the customer-employee interaction is critical for improving profit and lifetime customer value.

Setting up the right metrics and outcomes for each team member allows the manager to role play to improve performance. Remember that you cannot script human interaction but you can role play scenarios and create solutions for each scenario. This is where trust and empowerment come into play. Customer loyalty begins when people with the right skills and training are leveraged in a position with the autonomy to create a winning solution for the customers' concerns. One additional side-effect is employee engagement. Humans strive for autonomy and setting up a framework in your organization to foster autonomy is the first step to increasing customer lifetime value and loyalty.

THE RESULT OF SOCIAL MEDIA

Before the Internet, there was a rule that happy customers shared their experiences with three people while unhappy customers would tell eleven people. In the age of social media, upset customers have an easily accessible forum to share their stories with millions of people.

> The band Sons of Maxwell was flying United Airlines to a gig in Nebraska. Dave Carroll checked his guitar at baggage. Witnesses saw handlers throwing bags around, including Dave's guitar, which sustained $1,200 in damage. For six months, Dave tried to remedy the situation and simply get his guitar fixed. The bureaucracy and lack of accountability that United Airlines offered was unacceptable. Dave ended up writing a song about the incident and publishing it on YouTube. This video has over 12 million views. Let's do some basic math and try to quantify this simple screw up. Instead of fixing or replacing Dave's guitar, United Airlines elected to fight the claim. Did they save money? YouTube does not track unique visits so let's assume that out of the 12 million views over the last three years, 3 million of them are unique. Now let's assume that the average roundtrip plane ticket is $300. This video has the propensity to keep customers away; so 3 million unique views times $300 each is $900 million. This also assumes that viewers are persuaded not to fly United or fly only once; however many people fly more frequently. A conservative estimate is this cost United Airlines $900

million versus fixing the problem for $1,200. Needless to say, disengaged team members have the potential to lose millions of dollars for an organization. United Airlines has had several quarters where they lost money and this incident shows us why.

THE IMPORTANCE OF MANAGING EMOTIONS

Company culture requires framing at the top and executing at the frontline through the management ranks. Aligning company metrics and outcomes with employee metrics and outcomes for each position fosters a culture of high performance. This will not happen if executive leadership does not believe it and trust its people.

Align team members with their roles and leverage the strengths of the individual with the tasks required for the role and you will create a high-performance culture. Southwest Airlines has one of the best company cultures. Southwest is the only airline in history to never lose money. It was also the only airline that did not raise fares and cut routes after 9/11. Southwest does not train happiness, it hires happy people. Executives understand that their customer-facing people need to be nice, happy, and bubbly. They train their team members on the organization's processes and methods but are smart enough to know that you cannot train people "to be a certain way." Southwest's financial report card speaks for itself. They are successful because they manage the emotions of their team members and customers better than any other airline.

CHAPTER 8
FAST TRACK TO SUCCESS

Team members need managers who know how to draw out talents and align talents with the specific tasks that are required to build great organizations. Leaders create the vision and lead the ship. They set the outward direction of the organization, which is essential for growth. Some believe management is a rung on the ladder leading to leadership, but these are separate functions. Management is inwardly focused on the team while leadership is focused outward.

Great managers listen, leverage peoples' strengths, understand that people want to be understood, pick the right people, and never over promote. Characteristic behavior of great managers is pretty straightforward. They make few promises, keep them all, and never pass

the buck. The goal is to leverage intellectual capital
toward maximum performance.

Performance requires definition for each team member.
Personal scorecards communicating what is expected
from each team member are vital so people understand
what maximum performance for their role actually
means. Most high-value tasks in today's working
environments are right-brain creative work. Talented
people are good at sensing, judging, creating, and
building relationships.

How do you measure great performance from the top
down? Some excellent indicators are sales/employee,
profit/employee, turnover, absenteeism, and shrinkage.
For public companies we look at Return on Equity, Sales
Growth Rate, Earnings per Share, Book Value per Share,
and Free Cash Flow. These indicators are good at
establishing a baseline for team member and
organizational performance. The performance measures
must align to the role and outcomes that are expected.

Let's examine three companies: Hershey, Intel, and Bank
of America. We will look at some baseline numbers that
value investors like Warren Buffet would use to rate
companies. (I use publically traded companies because
the numbers are easy to find and compare.)

1. **Return on Equity:** This is basically the return you get back from the cash you've invested into the business. Anything over 10% is worth considering for a value investor.

2. **Sales Growth Rate:** This shows how much sales grow year after year.

3. **Earnings per Share Growth Rate:** This is how much the business is profiting per share of ownership. The growth rate compares year to year. It should increase 10% or more.

4. **Sales per Employee:** This is the sales revenue per employee.

5. **Profit per Employee**: This is the profit per employee.

The Hershey Company

Return on Equity: 64.83% (industry average is 22.05%)

Sales Growth Rate: 7%

Sales per Employee: $537,110 (industry average is $411,000)

Profit per Employee: $57,048 (industry average is $34,700)

Summary: In 2011, the Hershey Company made $962.85 million on $6.08 billion in sales. Amazon made $934 million on $48.08 billion in sales. Needless to say, Hershey is a well-run company.

Intel Corp

Return on Equity: 25.42%

Sales Growth Rate: 25%

Sales per Employee: $544,725 (industry average is $463,000)

Profit per Employee: $123,806 (industry average is $87,106)

Summary: In 2011, Intel made $12.39 billion on $54.53 billion in sales. Their sales grew 25% last year. This company is very well-run.

Bank of America

Return on Equity: 4.67% (value investors look for 10% or higher)

Sales Growth Rate: -15%

Sales per Employee: $326,132 (industry average is $310,725)

Profit per Employee: $5,046 (industry average is $47,640)

Summary: Bank of America is not performing like the other two companies above.

These numbers are the macro indicators that tell a story on overall company performance. How do employees know what their effectiveness is as it relates to these numbers? Employee scorecards need to measure what each person can control. Those measures have to roll up and affect the bottom-line results.

A core human need is to be trusted. Great managers understand this and foster trust with their people.

Insecure and controlling managers cause lots of headaches and employee turnover. Most of the time people will execute a task different than you would. Micro-managers cause undue stress within the team and create barriers to creative problem-solving. Typically, controlling managers justify their actions because without their scrutiny, the people will take advantage of the situation to not work. This is a common misperception with autonomy. People, in general, want freedom to control their work environment and schedule.

> I have twin one-year-old daughters. They are starting to walk and get mobile. If you try to restrain them for any length of time, your ears get punished. It is an inherent human need to be free and explore. Trying to restrain freedom causes conflict and kills innovation. Now, the need to set parameters for the twin's safety is very important. Set parameters and expectations for team members and let them run.

This is especially true for right-brain creative work. Controlling managers have a problem with allowing this because they do not trust the employee. This also shows one glaring flaw of the manager. If you have to control the behavior of your people and micromanage them, accountability, metrics, and outcomes are not clearly defined. When these basics are not outlined, insecurity will rear its ugly head and controlling behavior is necessary to get anything done.

> Throughout my career, I have seen managers and key employees work hard. Their need for job security required them to work many hours and not share the workload. This is common in small companies and small departments within larger companies. People fear losing their job so they do a lot of work and don't share the knowledge. I have dealt with this in sales, service, development, and administration. This was bad management on my part until I realized what was really happening. I did not do a good job of laying out the vision and the growth potential for the people. Great managers strive to eliminate their jobs. This means that the team runs so well that they no longer have to manage it. This is truly a goal all managers should strive for because when it happens the responsibilities grow as well. With this insight, I was able to communicate it to my people. Knowledge and work was shared and revenues grew. My people expanded their knowledge and have more responsibility and are able to handle the responsibility as a team. You cannot run to home plate if your foot is still stuck on first base. Additionally, this behavior costs lots of money and wasted time and took me too long to fix. Do yourself a favor and fix it now if you identify it as being a problem.

In the book *First, Break All The Rules,* Marcus Buckingham and Curt Coffman review the twelve statements below. These are an excellent barometer of what requires improvement or change in your organization. Each statement has deep meaning and they build on each other. These should be given to your team members as an anonymous survey. Answers are ranked on a scale of 1 to 5 with 1 meaning Strongly Disagree and 5 meaning Strongly Agree.

1. I know what is expected of me at work.

2. I have the materials and equipment I need to do my job right.

3. At work, I have the opportunity to do what I do best every day.

4. In the last seven days, I have received recognition or praise for doing good work.

5. My supervisor, or someone at work, seems to care about me as a person.

6. There is someone at work who encourages my development.

7. At work, my opinions seem to count.

8. The mission/purpose of my company makes me feel my job is important.

9. My coworkers are committed to doing quality work.

10. I have a best friend at work.

11. In the last six months, someone at work has talked to me about my progress.

12. This last year, I had opportunities to learn and grow at work.

These statements follow Maslow's Hierarchy of Needs. Humans have an inherent need for belonging. The idea is to align and obtain what I call organizational-actualization. At the top of Maslow's Hierarchy, is self-enlightenment or self-actualization. Imagine when the collective achieves that level en masse. Then compound the collective with organizational-actualization and you have the making of a great company.

In order to achieve this, managers must work with their direct reports daily on fostering their talents and managing through their weaknesses. I can tell you from experience that hiring the wrong people is the biggest energy and cash drain on a company.

Remember you cannot have customer loyalty without team member engagement. To have engagement you need to align innate talents with performance outcomes of the roles.

REASONING BEHIND THE 12 STATEMENTS

1.   I know what is expected of me at work.

This is critical, especially for new hires. Disengagement happens when an employee first considers leaving the company. When you have a talented engaged employee, you want to keep him in that state. Remember that turnover costs roughly 1.5 times the salary of the person being replaced. Managers and employees alike should push each other to make sure expectations are concrete and in writing. This means that employee knows what to measure each day, what they are striving to master, and the purpose of their roles.

2.   I have the materials and equipment I need to do my job right.

Having the tools to do a job right is essential and exciting. You can see that if the response to the first statement is negative, then defining "right" in statement two does not mean anything because the employee and manager have not agreed on what is right.

3.   I have the opportunity to do what I do best every day.

One staple of employee engagement is allowing employees to be more of what they already are. Remember one of the key points of a great manager is to "try to draw out what was left in." This means that you need to let employees leverage their innate talents to execute their roles. When this happens, your people will more likely enter flow states that create and sustain engagement.

> 4. *In the last seven days, I have received recognition or praise for doing good work.*

There have been various studies that show money is not the main motivator for good work and that the number one reason people leave is because of their direct supervisor. One key element is recognition. The frequency of seven days is suggested because people need affirmation that they are doing good work. Obviously the recognition has to be genuine or it means nothing. One of Maslow's defined needs is that of belonging. People need to know that they belong to something and that they are cared about. Recognition is a core component in satisfying that need.

> 5. *My supervisor, or someone else at work, seems to care about me as a person.*

This builds on the previous statements and strives to satisfy the core human need of wanting to be loved, accepted, and acknowledged.

6. *There is someone at work who encourages my development.*

Skills and knowledge can be taught. Human development at work is important because if you are not growing then you are slowly stagnating. There is no equilibrium because business is always changing and evolving. To encourage development and employee growth, companies can establish apprenticeships and mentoring programs. (The best approach to mastering most skills is to be mentored.)

7. *My opinions seem to count at work.*

This is a classic indicator of disengagement. When people feel like their opinions mean nothing, they will disengage. When companies stifle opinions because management is controlling and not trusting, creativity is destroyed. Great managers are excellent listeners and they understand that employee engagement leads to customer loyalty and listening to their team's opinions is vitally important.

8. The mission/purpose of my company makes me feel my job is important.

If management does not communicate to its team why each job is important, members will become disengaged. Each role in every company exists for a reason. Those reasons need to be communicated to the people in the roles. Every person's actions affect someone in the company. Think about a busboy in a restaurant. This may seem like a thankless job but a smart waitress knows that if she takes care of the busboy then her tips will escalate. The mission/purpose of the company needs to align with the values of the person.

9. My coworkers are committed to doing quality work.

Framing performance above feelings is important for the whole team. The quickest way for managers to demotivate a productive, engaged team is to allow certain team members to underperform. One benefit of this process is that the emotion of discipline is taken out when everybody knows what is expected of them.

10. I have a best friend at work.

Humans spend 30% of their lives at work. Do you want to spend that time with people you don't like? If you have a conflict with a neighbor, would you invite him over for dinner? Why would anybody want to spend their time with people they don't like? Having a best friend at work fosters employee engagement. Great managers know that people leave because of their direct associations with coworkers and managers. If people feel like they do not belong, they will leave. You want your people to have best friends at work since it bonds the team and the company and inherently helps create engagement.

> *11. In the last six months, someone at work has talked to me about my progress.*

Performance requires measurement. Reviewing performance every six months or less is a valuable exercise. Ideally, if the right measurements and automation are in place, managers can see performance at a glance and discuss progress weekly.

> *12. This last year, I had opportunities to learn and grow at work.*

Learning is a lifelong pursuit. Learning organizations deliver on results and are best of breed. I am very passionate about this because traditional education has done a good job of demotivating people to learn. The statistics are staggering and show that once people complete their schooling, they read maybe one to five books during the remainder of their lives. This is a flawed mentality and organizations need to foster continuous learning.

There are many learning styles an organization may select, but if the organization does not have an encouraged learning policy, your people will stagnate and so will growth. I attribute all of our success to learning. The people in our organization who are committed to learning outperform the non-learners by a wide margin. If your organization scores low on this statement, you need to re-evaluate and create a learning framework. Information is exploding and competitors will eat your lunch if your organization is not evolving and learning. All of these questions are vitally important but this one determines greatness or mediocrity.

CHAPTER 9
TALENT

What talents are required for each job? Knowing this upfront is critical. Realize there is a difference between talent, knowledge, and skill. Talent is not taught. You either have talent or you don't. Skills and knowledge can be taught and learned and are a vital part to an employee's growth. Successful organizations outperform their peers because they enhance skills and knowledge and, through learning, draw out talent and align it effectively. The best way to describe the differences between talent, knowledge, and skill is by examining professional football.

Barry Sanders is a legendary running back who played for the Detroit Lions. He was one of the best and his talents were unbelievable. His running methods, reactions, and agility were the best in professional football. His talent fit the role of a running back. Barry Sanders could not play linebacker, defensive tackle, or center. He simply did not have the stature or innate talent to play those positions. His skills and knowledge grew as he moved from the college to the pro level. His understanding of defenses, formations, and blitzing strategies are examples of enhanced skill and knowledge. His continuous learning and enhancement of his skills and knowledge allowed him to enhance his innate talent.

Now, I could acquire Barry's skills and knowledge of the game through hard work, study, and dedication but there is no way I could have played his position. I simply do not have the talent. This simple analogy gives us great insights into team management as well as individual management requirements.

Consider your team. Are all members in the right positions? Do they have innate talents that are leveraged to achieve the performance outcomes required? Until resolved, these are the questions that keep great managers up at night.

One thing that is absolutely essential is the definition of the required performance outcome for EVERY role in the organization. This is not a job description. Investing the time to truly define what is expected and what talents are required for each position is the best investment.

This is not always easy to do but one way to start is to look at your best people right now. Do you have an outstanding software developer? What innate talents does he have? Study your best people and then scale those talents to grow. As an example, let's review the talents required for a great software developer compared to those of a great salesperson.

Characteristic talents required of a great software developer:

1. Highly analytical

2. Does not procrastinate

3. Skeptical and questioning to get to the root cause of issues

4. Able to see code in their head

5. Passionate about coding and spends free time tinkering with software

6. Wants to write code not manage people

7. Dislikes bureaucracy

8. Impatient and strong-willed toward problem solving

Understanding people's habits is important in uncovering their innate talents. Simple questions like what do you enjoy doing in your free time are helpful. When I ask this question in interviews, if they are not building websites or applications or games then they probably don't love coding.

Characteristic talents required of a great salesperson:

1. Not paralyzed by fear

2. Tackles challenges

3. Does not procrastinate

4. Asks tough questions to get to the root cause of issues

5. Hates losing more than they like winning

6. Outstanding listener

7. Very decisive

8. Understands the power of silence

9. Great communicator and storyteller. Can present to groups and is comfortable being in front of people.

10. Great detective. Strives to understand the workings of a deal and views it as a chess match.

What happens if the sales type was cast in the development role and the developer type was cast in a sales role? Each would crash and burn and the performance outcomes would be dismal. This is no different than trying to cast Barry Sanders as a defensive tackle. The innate talents must fit the role.

The two examples above are pretty easy to decipher but other roles are not as obvious. This is why great managers study their best people and understand the talents required for each role that reports to them.

Organizations that learn to leverage the strengths and talents of their team members outperform those that don't. There have been countless research projects that show this, including examples in *Good to Great* by Jim Collins and *Less is More* by Jason Jennings. These books show conclusively that leadership and team member engagement fosters customer loyalty.

How do you identify talents and strengths? Gallup has done extensive study on the topic and has created a proprietary system outlining 34 core talents by using the StrengthsFinder test. There are other personality tests, like DiSC and Myers Briggs. Any of these are good tools to use when trying to place the right people.

Innate talents are hardwired into people. You cannot change them, as illustrated in the following short story:

Scorpion: Are you going to cross the pond sometime today?

Frog: I was thinking about it. I probably will.

Scorpion: Can I get a ride on your back to get across? I cannot swim.

Frog: No way, you will sting me and I will die.

Scorpion: Hey, wait a minute. You are not thinking with your frog brain. If I sting you and you drown then I drown and die. Why would I do that?

The frog ponders the thought.

Frog: Okay. Get on.

In the middle of the pond, the scorpion stings the frog.

Frog: Why did you do that? We are both going to die.

Scorpion: I can't help it. I am scorpion and that is my nature.

Understanding each person's wiring and recurring habits will give you insight into their talents. I have focused on positive talents but people have negative or counterproductive talents that require understanding as well. For example, some high-performing salespeople have giant egos and act like prima donnas. They are cowboys at heart and this behavior is disturbing to the rest of the team. Great managers understand how to manage through this and they also realize that if the behavior is too destructive then they need to fire them. Likewise, great software developers have little patience and can be abrupt and resistant to other ideas. This can stifle the team if not kept in check.

For example, the mindset that all software is horrible if it is not developed in-house is a bad talent if not kept in check. In this scenario, *great* can be the enemy of progress. A perfectionist mindset can keep the software in permanent beta which results in fiscal disaster.

Great managers align the right people with the right roles and communicate the meaning of the role to the employee and give them performance measures that make sense. Great managers understand these tenants:

1. People do not change much.

2. Don't waste time trying to put in what was left out.

3. Try to draw out what was left in.

4. Number 3 is the hard part.

Leveraging positive talents and managing around weaknesses to hit performance outcomes are the key ingredients to building a great organization.

People have their own unique filters. Filters are perceptions. Great trial lawyers understand this and typically can question two eye witnesses and get different stories. Perceptions are as unique as fingerprints. Filters help identify talents as well as weaknesses.

Mindset is a big part of perception. Southwest Airlines makes it mandatory to hire nice, positive, friendly, bubbly people. These traits are filters—just like skeptical, negative, and confrontational are. All of these attitudes can be effective if they are in the right role. I would much rather have my financial people be skeptical, questioning, and confrontational with my money instead of friendly, nice, and giving.

Motivational drive is a perception and mindset. It cannot be taught. If people want to change their attitudes, they have to take the initiative. Nobody else can do it for them. This is critical to understand because companies waste time and money trying to change employee mindsets. Most performance reviews focus on the weaknesses of the employee over the last six months. This becomes a dumping ground for what they did wrong and how they need to improve in weak areas. This framework is upside down and a waste of time. Great managers know they need to invest their time with their best people and foster strengths and manage through weaknesses.

Managers in today's market spend a ton of time trying to improve weaknesses. This comes from the old manufacturing management methods. If you consider TQM (Total Quality Management) then you understand that manufacturing and processes are streamlined to maximize efficiency and quality. These measures work great for processes but not for people.

> By nature, I am not a highly detailed person. I am more bottom-line, big picture oriented. If I am given a stack of invoices and required to code them into the accounting system this task is leveraging my weaknesses. I would sit in meetings with my manager reviewing my mistakes and slow progress. This task does not fit my innate talents and over time frustration levels for me and the company would show. Now, I may not communicate this problem because

based on my hierarchy of needs, I have to eat. Eating is required before self-actualization.

In this economy, employees are not going to willfully tell you that they hate the tasks they are asked to do. Over time the performance will show that they are not good at it but humans are programmed to survive. If you look around your organization, you understand that there are people who do just enough to not get fired. This was highlighted in a great movie called *Office Space*. These workers were actively disengaged and did just enough to not get fired. Not correcting this can destroy the company.

Uncovering talents is a key requirement for managers. Asking questions is a critical first step. Ask questions about passions, free time, activities, likes, dislikes, travel, previous experiences, and schooling. Remember that people's perceptions are their realities; so, the more you understand and investigate the better your chances at uncovering innate talents.

As you may have guessed, understanding your people means you need to know them. Some management philosophy disagrees with getting too personal with your direct reports. Great managers disagree. They know that in order to get the best from each of their employees, they need to know what makes them tick. (I discussed this earlier in Chapter 2.) Habits are recurring behaviors and are indicators of talent. Understanding the recurring behaviors of your people will indicate if they are in line with the role or out of line with the role. This also explains why you need to understand what habits complement each role.

CHAPTER 10
THE PETER PRINCIPLE

Continuous learning requires consistent practice by
every team member every day. The consequences of not
doing this result in the Peter Principle. Dr. Lawrence J.
Peter was a scientist who studied incompetence. The
Peter Principle simply states that in organizations, people
tend to rise to their level of incompetence. They tend to
stay in that position throughout their career. Let's look
at some examples. (The names and companies are
changed to protect the guilty.)

> Early in my career, we were looking for additional revenue
> streams for growth. We figured we would sell digital InCar
> Video to police departments. The 30 seconds of thought
> given to this decision was that we were already selling to
> this market. I figured we could leverage the customer base
> and increase the value for them and us alike.

In our business, sales/marketing, service/support and administration must work together and be educated on a new product and market in order to deliver it. Of course, I learned the ramifications of this AFTER we decided to sell InCar Video. I was in such a hurry that we simply looked at a couple of products to resell and picked one. Then we bought our demo system and were off to the races.

I am sure you can already see the incompetence, but let me highlight it with a sledge hammer. When we sold the product, none of us had any idea on the installation and ongoing service that was involved in a successful implementation. I took the Ready and Fire approach and had no regard for AIM. My techs were not prepared to deliver to the customer and it showed.

The results were pretty horrific. With this brilliant idea of mine, we were able to upset a few of our good customers because we sold them this solution, upset our technical installers because we did not allocate the right resources, and lost a bunch of money. The good news is that we are no longer in this market.

Let me specify the areas I was incompetent in with this decision.

1. Not being allowed to scale and grow as a reseller.

2. Not providing adequate capital to deliver
   properly.

3. Not doing any market gap analysis to see if we
   could provide value and make money.

4. Not talking to other companies outside our
   geography to see how successfully they
   delivered.

5. Jumping off the diving board before knowing the
   pool had water in it.

This story bleeds incompetence and Dr. Peter argues that
everybody in a hierarchy is promoted to their level of
incompetence. There is an inherent disconnect because
people want to be elevated in their career. Typically
incompetence happens when managers and employees
alike do not understand the ramifications of the new
position.

A professional baseball pitcher does not make a good
pitching coach. These two positions are totally different
yet the pitcher gets promoted time and time again after
his career. This is seen in sales as well. Typically you
have a high-producing sales professional who
continuously meets and exceeds goals. Management
sees this effectiveness and figures this salesperson would

make a good sales manager. If he can sell this much, then he can get the whole team selling more.

Why does this breed incompetence? The innate talents, skills, and knowledge between sales and management are totally different. When you are a hunting salesperson, your job is to find and get new business. You control your schedule, your time, and your activity. The position calls for prospecting, presentations, qualifying prospects, storytelling, and asking difficult questions to ultimately win the deal and create a new customer. Sales management requires team building, listening, doing work to help your team, coaching, and being with each team member.

> Earlier in my career, I purchased a company and acquired additional salespeople and accounts. I needed help with managing this division's sales department. I asked one of my good salespeople if he would be interested in doing the job. He agreed. I did this out of necessity, trust, and laziness. Since growing sales was not our company's strong point, I was hesitant to hire a new competent sales manager.
>
> The result of this simple change in responsibilities resulted in a frustrated sales team and sales manager. The outcomes were dismal. We lost a good salesperson because the manager was not getting the job done. We lost sales that the manager used to make because he was

too busy being incompetent as a sales manager. And, we lost the sales manager who went back into sales for another company.

Before I discuss how to avoid this, I want to share one more story to prove incompetence shows up everywhere.

My dad worked for General Motors in the early 1960s. Back then, having this job meant you could work there for thirty years and retire with a full pension. As a warehouse distribution assistant manager, he noticed that orders were not being filled for the spare parts. The warehouse was full of 20+-year-old parts and the customers asking for the parts were very frustrated. When he inquired about the problem, he was put off by management. They did not want to upset the hierarchy and bring attention to their area. My dad started fulfilling the orders and all hell broke loose. The incompetent people in this process were reprimanded and the warehouse became the most profitable one in the company.

The second level of incompetence came later in my dad's GM career. He received a phone call from an upset manager asking if he was going to accept the job he was offered. My dad had no idea he had been offered a different job at GM. Come to find out, his direct manager did not share several job offerings with my dad. He did not want to lose a competent worker because my father had the responsibility of three jobs. Once my dad found this out, he immediately resigned from the company. This was a huge risk because he had two kids and a third on the way. My grandfather blew a head gasket when he found out what my father had done. Back then, an automotive job was the Holy Grail of careers. It turned out to be the best decision my dad ever made because he became a highly successful serial entrepreneur. One of the corollaries to the Peter Principle is people will leave the hierarchy and not live with the incompetence.

How can organizations avoid the Peter Principle? First, you need to establish the correct outcomes for every position in your organization. This is critical and typically the primary cause of hierarchal incompetence. This is more than a job description. Each position has to be defined and measured in terms of outcomes and meaning to the rest of the organization. The innate talents, skills, and knowledge also require defining.

Second, realize that most people want to be promoted. There is a desire to progress. Jim Rohn summed it up like this:

"To get more, you need to become more."

Once organizations understand this they can manage around the Peter Principle.

Third, each role, once filled, is measured daily. You can't manage what you can't measure. All roles exist for established metrics and outcomes and they must have meaning and perform a desired outcome. If this is not the case, the role needs to be eliminated.

As organizations grow and become successful, this becomes harder to execute. Digital Equipment Corporation (DEC) was a highly successful mini-computer manufacturer. They had a policy of never laying people off and they were proud of it. This was an easy policy to enforce because they were executing and making money. As time went on, the market changed and they started slipping. They kept to their promise of not laying off workers. This policy, along with market conditions, ended DEC's rise and they were purchased by Compaq Computer (now HP).

Organizations and team members alike need to do their best to avoid the Peter Principle. Defining outcomes and establishing a learning organization will help in this endeavor.

CHAPTER 11
RETAINING CUSTOMER LOYALTY

Customer satisfaction is a stepping stone to customer loyalty which is needed to acquire repeat sales and referrals. To help you determine how your organization rates in customer satisfaction when selling to consumers, ask your customers to answer the following questions. The answers to this customer-engagement survey created by Gallup[6] will provide you the information you need to foster customer loyalty.

1. Taking into account all the products and services you receive from (Company), how satisfied are you with (Company) overall?

2. How likely are you to continue to do business with (Company)?

---

[6] Gallup, *Majority of Workers Not Engaged in Their Jobs*

3. How likely are you to recommend (Company) to a friend or associate?

4. (Company) is a name I can always trust.

5. (Company) always delivers on what they promise.

6. (Company) always treats me fairly.

7. If a problem arises, I can always count on (Company) to reach a fair and satisfactory resolution.

8. I feel proud to be a (Company) customer.

9. (Company) always treats me with respect.

10. (Company) is the perfect company/product for people like me.

11. I can't imagine a world without (Company).

12. Taking into account all the products and services you receive from (Company), how satisfied are you with (Company) overall?

This is a general question that uncovers if you are delivering the basics, like quality products and services.

The answers will identify any problems in your delivery chain. Definitely provide space for comments so customers can write about their experiences. If the experience is positive, then you can expand on those offerings and if something is bad, it gives you the opportunity to fix it. Trending this question over time is important to make sure you are continually delivering on the basics.

How likely are you to continue to do business with (Company)?

Repeat sales are a strong indicator of company strength; this question identifies any gaps. On average, the cost of acquiring a new customer is six times more costly then upselling or cross-selling an existing customer. Trending this question over time is critical for businesses to know how they are doing with Lifetime Customer Value.

How likely are you to recommend (Company) to a friend or associate?

The first indicator of customer loyalty is a person's ability to refer business. Referrals are one of the most powerful ways to achieve organic growth. Marketing departments need to trend referrals over time across all communication channels.

(Company) is a name I can always trust.

Trust is the bedrock foundation required for customer loyalty and maximizing Lifetime Customer Value. Customer loyalty is defined by customers referring business, repeat sales, and accepting minor glitches. Satisfied customers will leave for a lower price while loyal customers will not. When customers trust you, they buy from you more often and refer more often.

(Company) always delivers on what they promise.

Nothing is stronger than your word. To deliver on a promise means the frontline team members must know what the customer was promised. Trending this question will shine light on any communication gaps within the organization.

(Company) always treats me fairly.

Being treated fairly is a core component of building relationships with your customers. People expect to be treated fairly during transactions, i.e., if there is a return item, customers expect to be able to return it without a hassle. Nordstrom's has an excellent return policy. The company knows that a small percentage will take advantage of the policy and that is built into the model. They also know the additional revenue received from this fair return policy is much stronger than the shrinkage. Trending this question over time identifies any policy problems.

If a problem arises, I can always count on (Company) to reach a fair and satisfactory resolution.

On the surface, this question seems redundant but actually goes deeper than policies. This shows that the frontline team members know how to handle issues fairly. Trending this question over time will identify any training gaps at the local level. If your organization has multiple locations, this question shows which locations are delivering and which ones are not.

I feel proud to be a (Company) customer.

People buy on emotions and pride is a strong emotion and bonds the customer to your organization. Typically when people are proud, they are talking about their kids, close friends, or close team members. Pride strengthens customer loyalty.

(Company) always treats me with respect.

This is a pass/fail question. It measures team-member performance and will identify any local weaknesses. If the response to this question is low then your company most likely has a systemic leadership problem. Team members emulate their managers and leaders. If customers are being treated with disrespect, there is a good chance management is treating team members with disrespect. If the trend on this question is low answers, serious work is required and leadership may need to be changed.

(Company) is the perfect company/product for people like me.

Bonding and rapport happen when people are alike and have similar values. If people identify with you then your organization is delivering value.

I can't imagine a world without (Company)

If trending is high on this question, your organization is doing well. Companies with high scores would be Southwest Airlines, Apple, and Amazon. These organizations have a cult-like following. Your bottom line will be cemented in profit if you get this question right.

Receiving high marks on this survey is not an easy task but it should be your goal.

BUSINESS-TO-BUSINESS (B2B) SELLING

If your organization sells to businesses rather than consumers, you will want to include these four questions in the survey:

1. (Company) has a clear understanding of our business issues.

2. (Company) has had a significant impact on our performance.

3. (Company) is an easy firm with which to do business.

4. I consider (Company's) representatives to be trusted advisors.

When businesses sell to other businesses there are three things at play. Businesses buy products and services to increase revenue, reduce costs, and/or mitigate risk. Those are the only reasons. Let's dive into these four survey questions focusing on B2B customers.

1. *(Company) has a clear understanding of our business issues.*

This question must have high marks otherwise your sales team is simply taking a horizontal market approach which is not sustainable over time because specialists in the vertical market will win every time. Trending for this question has to be high out of the gate.

2. *(Company) has had a significant impact on our business performance.*

Providing services that increase revenue and reduce costs inherently impact performance in a positive way. The larger the hard-dollar impact, the better. Soft-dollar ROI (Return on Investment) calculations are harder to sell. When customers give high scores here, you are delivering well and likely to create a long-term customer. When organizations impact business value they tend to keep doing business together.

3. *(Company) is an easy firm with which to do business.*

Business customers want long-term partners that provide value; not vendors. Partners understand that a working relationship needs to be easy and flexible. Customer loyalty is built on partnerships not vendor/buyer transactions. High marks on this question prove that your organization understands partnerships.

4. I consider (Company's) representatives to be trusted advisors.

This is the Holy Grail of B2B relationships. If your organization receives high marks on this question, you are delivering value and you have a loyal customer. When you are a trusted advisor, lifetime value increases significantly. Trusted advisors significantly outsell vendors. Vendors usually try to win business on price because they are not viewed as trusted advisors. When you are a trusted advisor you will get repeat business without the headache of a convoluted buying cycle.

There is one last question I think is critically important and should be asked of every customer. It is the ultimate litmus test for customer loyalty:

Knowing what you know now, would you buy from (Company) again? Why or why not?

The answer to this question will shed light on how your organization is doing from the customer's point of view.

CONCLUSION

Customer loyalty is the goal of a business. I am not
talking about customer satisfaction. Satisfied customers
may buy Allstate Insurance today and switch to State
Farm tomorrow. Loyal customers will not do that.
Loyal customers do three things that are worth their
weight in gold: they buy more and their Lifetime Value
is higher than regular customers, they forgive mistakes,
and they refer new customers.

> *The purpose of a business is to gain a customer.*
> *- Peter Drucker*

I want to add *"profitable customer"* to this quote. Profit
is the motivation to create shareholder value and allows
businesses to exist. Two key aspects to a growing
business are innovation and marketing. Customers
become loyal when you have a great product or service
and you provide value. If you do not do this then

marketing becomes a sales pitch and loses its effectiveness. When you create real value, your business will grow.

Most pediatricians are trusted advisors. I can tell you from my experience with twin babies that our pediatrician is absolutely a trusted advisor. Are you a trusted advisor to your customers? When you are seen as a trusted advisor, you will create loyal customers.

Client loyalty must be measured because revenue growth is a company responsibility not only a sales responsibility. There is no faster way to grow revenue than by creating loyal customers.

The greatest businesses in the world have innovative and outstanding products / services and excellent marketing. These two factors are what allow businesses to acquire customers. Once those prospects become customers then it is the business team with engaged employees that turn them from customer to loyal customer.

How many businesses spend money on advertising to gain a new customer? One of the largest expenses for business is the cost of acquiring new customers. Customer acquisition costs usually are not measured by most organizations. This is a mistake. Understanding the true cost of acquiring a new customer dictates how fast you can grow.

The ratio cost difference between gaining a new customer and selling to an existing one is roughly 7 to 1. Focusing too much time on acquiring new business without catering to existing business is a problem for most businesses.

I have a good friend who runs a very successful dental practice. His focus is new patients. Each year he has grown the practice and his patient base has expanded as well. As most business people know, growth eats capital. It costs money to service new clients. My friend got exactly what he focused on, which was more production. The problem arose when existing customers who spend more money were pushed to the associate dentist. He found out the hard way that more production/patients equated to less profit.

We talked about this problem and we dug into what he was doing for his existing patients. His practice always provides great services but he was doing nothing to cater to the existing base. Let's put some numbers to this story so we can articulate the importance of loyal customers who spread the word.

His cost of customer acquisition is roughly $200 per patient gained. This means that he needs to see them twice before he makes a profit. Since there was no formal system for encouraging loyal customers to spread the word, this became a problem.

The difference in bottom line profit from selling to an existing patient is roughly $28.50 compared to the new patient at $200. When the $28.50 loyal patient tells her friend, the cost of that referral is $0. If you multiply this by 1000 patients the money saved is $171,500. It pays to focus on loyalty.

We have talked at great length on team member engagement and client loyalty. As you know you cannot have one without the other. When both are synergistically aligned, client loyalty and higher profit become a reality.

APPENDIX A
STOP-DOING MATRIX™

Markets, customers, and technology are dynamic and always changing. To keep team members engaged and productive, have them fill out the Stop-Doing Matrix™. This tool is designed for them to track their activity and their love/hate for the activity.

This is useful in keeping the employee engaged. Employees should do this for one full week and log every task they do. Things will show up that surprise the team member and direct supervisor.

You want to make sure that team members are engaging in high-productivity tasks they enjoy. You also need to understand that every job has tasks that are NOT enjoyable. The idea is to not have those tasks encompass 80% of the employee's time.

Stop Doing/Productive tool also acts as an early warning sign to employee disengagement. If the strength/weakness percentage is low know that the employee does not like what he is doing and changes may need to be made.

S/W	Rank	Productivity	Rank
1.	Task 1	5	4
2.	Task 2	4	5
3.	Task 3	2	3
4.	Task 4	2	5
5.	Task 5	5	5
Total points		18/25	22/25
Total Score		72%	88%

APPENDIX B
ELEARNING

ELearning systems are a powerful way to deliver content to your team members. An effective system ties performance to content. Being able to measure training effectiveness is important when using an ELearning system. When you look at virtual systems like Khan Academy (www.khanacademy.org) and Coursera (www.coursera.org), you will see that virtual learning is becoming mainstream.

You will also notice that these systems have to be extremely easy to use or people will not adopt them. ELearning has the potential to transform organizations. Proper learning systems will allow for trending of your team members over time as you are able to see exactly which team members are progressing and what skills are enhanced. This allows visibility for other team members to leverage skills and talents needed for projects. A functional ELearning system provides transparency and improvement across the organization skills, knowledge, and talents.

APPENDIX C
HIRING THE RIGHT PEOPLE

I am not an HR expert and by no means a hiring guru. With that said, I want to profile some things you can do to make sure new hires are right for your team. First, you need to fully understand what you want from the position being filled. This is much more than a job description. You need to know what strengths, talents, knowledge, and skills required to deliver excellent performance. Likewise, you need to know what weaknesses will kill performance in the position. If you need an offensive guard in football, you will not hire a quarterback. I know this seems obvious but common sense is not always that common. Let me outline this in business terms.

If your company does $25 million dollars in sales and you need to fill a Director of Sales position, would you hire a candidate who managed a billion dollar division?

You may be enticed to say yes but I would advise against it. People who work in billon dollar companies have many resources and transitioning to an entrepreneurial firm doing $25 million in sales could cause them frustration.

Second, make sure you perform several interviews and ask tough questions like:

What are your career goals?

This question will give insight into what the candidate wants to do. You will also know very quickly if their growth goals are in line with what you can provide.

What are you really good at professionally?

This question will give insight into what their strengths are. Since you know what you are looking for in the position, you will be able to identify very quickly if you should continue to evaluate this candidate.

What are you not good at or not interested in doing professionally?

This question will give you insight into their dislikes and weaknesses. You are keeping the question strictly at a professional level; not personal. If their weakness is a strength you need in the position then you know not to proceed with this candidate.

Who were your last three bosses and how will they each rate your performance on a 1-10 scale when I talk with them?

This question lets the candidate know you expect to talk with the last three employers. If the candidate hesitates to provide you with his last three bosses this signifies a red flag. You need to dig in and find out why. Once I started to ask this question in interviews, our hiring method improved dramatically.

Always go deeper and ask what, how, and tell me more.

Active listening and reversing are vital when interviewing candidates. Reversing is a simple technique of asking for more information. When a candidate gives you an answer, simply say "can you be more specific?" This will keep candidates talking. Remember in your initial interview, you want them talking about relevant information.

What were you hired to do at your last job?

This is a simple question that yields good insight. You will be able to evaluate their communication style.

What accomplishments are you most proud of?

Ask this for each job that the candidate has on his resume. This will give you additional exposure to his strengths.

What were some low points during that job?

Understanding weaknesses is just as important as knowing the strengths.

If you are interviewing for a management or team leader position, also ask these questions as they start getting to the heart of the matter and reinforce that you will contact their previous bosses.

What was your boss's name, and how do you spell it?

What was it like working with him/her?

What will he/she tell me are your biggest strengths and areas that need improvement?

These questions expose a ton of information. You will understand the candidate's level of accountability. You will understand if they hired or fired anybody and why. This gives insight into their daily behavior and interactions in a team environment. Knowing why they left the job is important. If the candidate jumps jobs often, this is a red flag.

How would you rate the team you inherited on a 1-10 scale?

What changes did you make?

Did you hire anybody?

Did you fire anybody?

How would you rate the team when you left it on a 1-10 scale?

Why did you leave that job?

If you have a large application pool, I recommend you perform telephone interviews and weed out most of the candidates. Also, search the social media sites (Facebook, Twitter, and LinkedIn) for any relevant information.

Have several team members interview candidates that make the short list. Make sure all your team members know the position requirements. They can ask the same questions outlined here. Once the interviews are complete, have a debriefing meeting and make sure the answers are the same. This seems redundant but the subtle differences in answers will shed a lot of light on the candidate.

Remember that you are bringing somebody in who has to fit into your company culture. You do not want to hire wrong and pollute a high-functioning team.

Your team members and customers deserve the best candidates so you need to take the time and hire correctly.

BIBLIOGRAPHY AND
RECOMMENDED READING

Blacksmith, Nikki and Harter, Jim. *Majority of American Workers Not Engaged in Their Jobs.* Gallup, Inc. 28 October 2011. www.gallup.com/poll/150383/majority-american-workers-not-engaged-jobs.aspx

Buckingham, Marcus and Coffman, Curt. *First, Break All the Rules: What the World's Greatest Managers Do Differently.* New York: Simon & Schuster, 1999.

Chapman, Gary D. *The 5 Love Languages: The Secret to Love That Lasts.* Northfield: Northfield Publishing, 2009.

Chapman, Gary D. and White, Paul E. *The 5 Languages of Appreciation in the Workplace: Empowering Organizations by Encouraging People.* Northfield: Northfield Publishing, 2012.

Clifton, Jim. *The Coming Jobs War.* Omaha: Gallup Press, 2011.

Collins, Jim. *Good to Great.* New York: HarperBusiness, 2001.

Csikszentmihalyi, Mihaly. *Finding Flow: The Psychology of Engagement with Everyday Life.* New York: Basic Books, 1998.

Csikszentmihalyi, Mihaly. *Flow: The Psychology of Optimal Experience* . New York: Harper Perennial Modern Classics (HarperCollins), 2008.

Frankl, Viktor E. *Man's Search for Meaning.* Boston: Beacon Press, 2006.

Hill, Napoleon. *Outwitting the Devil: The Secret to Freedom and Success.* New York: Sterling, 2012.

Hill, Napoleon. *Think and Grow Rich. The Original 1937 Unedited Edition.* Wise, VA: Napoleon Hill Foundation, 2012.

Hill, Napoleon. *The Master Key to Riches (Dover Empower Your Life).* Mineola: Dover Publications, 2009.

Hill, Napoleon. *The Law of Success: The Master Wealth-Builder's Complete and Original Lesson Plan for Achieving Your Dreams.* New York: Tarcher, 2008.

Jennings, Jason. *Less Is More: How Great Companies Use Productivity.* New York: Portfolio Hardcover, 2002.

Lencioni, Patrick. *The Three Signs of a Miserable Job: A Fable for Managers (And Their Employees).* Hoboken: Jossey-Bass, 2007.

Loehr, Jim and Schwartz, Tony. *The Power of Full Engagement: Managing Energy, Not Time, Is the Key to High Performance and Personal Renewal.* New York: Free Press (Simon & Schuster), 2004.

Medina, John. *Brain Rules*. Seattle: Pear Press, 2009.

Olson, Jeff. *The Slight Edge*. Atlanta: Success Books, 2011.

Pink, Daniel H. *Drive: The Surprising Truth About What Motivates Us*. New York: Riverhead Books (Penguin Group USA), 2011.

Young, Robert O. and Young, Shelley Redford. *Sick and Tired?: Reclaim Your Inner Terrain*. Salt Lake City: Woodland Publishing, 2000.

Judge, Mike, Director. *Office Space*. (1999).

CPSIA information can be obtained
at www.ICGtesting.com
Printed in the USA
FFOW03n1632251116

9 781933 598796